Positive Reviews from Readers
Everything I Wish I Knew When I

"I enjoyed your book, *All the Things I Wish I Knew When I w.* students and staff. At least now I know I am not alone when, no matter what I do, I cannot please everybody. All the books you have authored I have looked over, and they all seem very informative and relevant. There are several new concepts that I have not seen before, as well as many that I have seen, but need to see over and over again anyway. Thank you for providing all your information."

Glenn Finke
Traditional Karate-Do Center
www.warwickkarate.com

"Your genius is the ability to see things from a perspective that virtually no one else does. Your combination of an MBA and 20 years pioneering ideas for professional martial arts instructors is a valuable treasure for school owners such as myself.

School owners have a choice of either spending 20 years in the process or trial and error coming up with new ideas, all the while wasting precious time and energy, plus thousands of dollars, or they can get the "Cliff Notes" to success, which are your *All the Things I Wish I Knew When I was 22* section of Extraordinary Marketing. That's a starting point to standing on the shoulders of your wisdom!"

Chris Rappold
Personal Best Karate (3 locations)
Norton, MA

"Stephen I have to say that I would have paid the fee just for your *All the Things I Wish I Knew When I was 22.* It was absolutely brilliant, and really forced me to think about my own set-up in the UK. I sat there reading it thinking, "This is me"! Many of the problems you highlighted I am currently dealing with myself, and your views were certainly a balanced and well thought-out comment on my current situation. Keep up the good work."

Stephen Cowley
Steve Cowley's Martial Arts Academy
High Wycombe, Bucks, United Kingdom

"I do want to thank you for marketing such an extraordinary package of materials. 'Awesome' is the only word I can use to describe your package at such a low cost. I have had an academy (six days a week) open for the last twelve years, and before that, worked for one of my instructors for about six years in his five schools. The reason that I say low cost (and you know what I am talking about), is that we have paid out thousands of dollars over the years for business ideas and teaching ideas!

The little book *All the Things I Wish I Knew When I was 22* was worth the cost of your program. Anyway, it has been the shot in the arm that we needed, and we thank you for the dose of medicine. Thanks for your program. Keep the faith, and keep plugging—"if you never give up, never quit and you never surrender, you will never fail. May the Lord God Almighty continue to bless and keep you and you family always, amen."

Gordon Dixon
Tupelo Martial Arts Academy
Shannon, MS

Continued on next page

"Our currency (Rand) is very weak in comparison to the Dollar. You can multiply the price by eighgt to have an idea what I paid for the product! I am still very happy that I had bought the program! Although we are worlds apart, the similarity of our markets is absolutely scary! I am currently reading through *All the Things I Wish I Knew When I was 22* for a second time, and really enjoy your aproach.

I am (was) a technical fighter and teacher all my life, and only loved Karate-do. I am now rapidly changing to become a marketer, seller, business person, etc. It had been an eye-opening experience to read the material you had sent. I am eagerly awaiting to apply nearly every single suggestion in the program. The similarity in our markets are really amazing! Although we are continents apart! I enjoyed the line, "I have not found even a single advantage into entering my students into the external tournaments". I am currently working through all the material and will have my web site, etc., in place for the beginning of our academic year, which is January. I will keep you posted!"

Soon Pretorius
Karate Academy of South Africa
Pretoria, Gauteng, South Africa

"Well, I have to admit—this is one of the first times I have read something from the many people who try to tell us how to run a school where the advice is obviously coming from someone who has.

We have been running a small group of successful schools for almost 25 years, and after that kind of experience, it is easier to tell the good advice from the bad."

Doug Adamson

Everything I Wish I Knew When I Was 22

By Stephen Oliver, MBA

Author's Note

This is version four of an on-going work that has been, and, continues to be, included as a part of the Extraordinary Marketing Program (along with *Using the Internet to Market Your Martial Arts School, Direct Response Marketing for Martial Arts Schools, One Idea Worth $500,000* and other resources and tools).

I have included this book in the start-up package for NAPMA Maximum Impact members for several reasons. First, the feedback that I've received from the hundred of school owners who have read it has been overwhelmingly positive, and in some cases, "life-changing." One customer—Lloyd Irvin—said that as he read this while in Brazil to compete, that it "kicked his butt," and illuminated his many mistakes and misdirection in the industry. Second, certain sections have been VERY controversial in certain segments of our industry. I will not discontinue in our future interactions my "Tell it Like It Is–Politically Incorrect Approach." Be WARNED: my intent is not to offend you or anyone else, but, I plan in the future to continue pointing out MYTHS and Misdirections that have perpetuated themselves throughout our industry. Third, I feel even to those of use who have learned these lessons through the "school of hard knocks," they bear reviewing and repeating, since many of us get seduced into repeating the mistakes of the past—or, even worse, discontinuing successes of the past.

About the Author

Stephen Oliver began martial arts training in 1969 in Tulsa, Oklahoma, at a branch school of the Jhoon Rhee Institute. He opened his first school in 1975. He later moved to Washington, D.C. to work for the Jhoon Rhee Institute first as an instructor, and later as their youngest-ever branch manager, while earning an honor's degree in Economics at Georgetown University.

In 1983, he moved to the Denver metropolitan area, and opened five schools in 18 months with only $10,000 in capital. He went on to promote the Mile High Karate Classic NASKA World tour event and serve on NASKA's Board of Directors from 1989–1999, and on EFC's Board of Directors from inception until 2002.

In 1992 he earned his Master's in Business Administration (MBA) from the University of Denver, and went on to serve on their Venture and Entrepreneurship Advisory Board. He has also written several other books including: H*ow to Market Your Martial Arts School Using the Internet* and *Direct Response Marketing for Martial Arts Schools*. He has been actively involved in NAPMA since before its inception, and has been an on-going and active contributor and speaker.

Currently, he is CEO and majority owner of Martial Arts Marketing, Incorporated, DBA National Association of Professional Martial Artists (NAPMA), and Martial Arts Professional Magazine (www.MartialArtsProfessional.com). He continues to focus on his Mile High Karate schools, which has "Regional Developers" in place throughout the world, and is the leading, and fastest-growing, professional Martial Arts School Franchise system (www.MileHighFranchise.com), with locations throughout the world. in the Denver area, he has nine locations, and continues to speak to and write for martial arts school operators throughout the world, as well as consult for a very select team of school owners.

He is currently an 8th-Degree Black Belt in American Tae Kwon Do, and oversees an organization that teaches a diverse range of martial arts styles.

"Everything I Wish I Knew When I Was 22"

By Stephen Oliver

ExtraordinaryMarketing
2555 East Jamison Avenue, Littleton, CO 80122; 303-740-2291, FAX: 303-796-7181
StephenOliver@ExtraordinaryMarketing.com | www.ExtraordinaryMarketing.com

Mailing Address: P.O. Box 260267, Lakewood, CO 80226
Phone: 1-800-795-2695; From outside North America: 1-303-740-9467
Email: StephenOliver@MileHighKarate.com | Facebook: www.Facebook.com/StephenOliver

Other Tools and Resources Available at www.MartialArtsResources.com

Contents

Chapter 1   The Great Fallacies When You Start Your Business 6
Chapter 2   The E-Myth.. 10
Chapter 3   Wealth vs. Lifestyle 12
Chapter 4   Figure Out What You LOVE First 16
Chapter 5   Everything is Negotiable... 18
Chapter 6   Fire Those who "Suck the Life" from Your School 22
Chapter 7   Separate Your Hobby from Your Business 26
Chapter 8   Manage Your Time, Live Your Life.. 28
Chapter 9   Bigger Isn't Always Better 32
Chapter 10   Networking Your Way to Everything You Need to Know............................. 34
Chapter 11   Always Protect Yourself First... 40
Chapter 12   Things are Never as Bad as You Think They Are.. 42
Chapter 13   Things are Never as Good as You Think They Are.. 44
Chapter 14   Landlords and Other People Who Want to Bleed You Dry............................ 46
Chapter 15   Don't Confuse Activity with Accomplishment... 48
Chapter 16   Simplify, Simplify, Simplify... 50
Chapter 17   Why Am I Doing This to Myself? 52
Chapter 18   Hiring from within 56
Chapter 19   Separate Your EGO from Your Business.. 57
Chapter 20   The 10 "Secrets" of Leadership... 60
Chapter 21   Open Book Management 63
Chapter 22   The Real Secrets of Wealth in a Martial Arts School.................................... 67
Chapter 23   Learn from the *Real* Experts... 70
Chapter 25   Always Follow the Money... 73
Chapter 25   Getting Rich Off the Blood of Your Employees 74
Chapter 26   Aligning Your Interests 76
Chapter 27   The "Dramatic Metamorphosis" Employee vs. Owner 78
Chapter 28   You Can't Teach a Pig to Sing.. 80
Chapter 29   Never Stop Learning... 82
Chapter 30   "Opinions are Like..., Everyone's Got One"... 84
Chapter 31   The Quickest Way to Kill a School 86
Chapter 32   "Be Careful What you Wish for...You May Get It," Part 1 89
Chapter 33   "Be Careful What You Wish for...You May Get It," Part 2 93
Chapter 34   Important Issues for Large Operators 97
Chapter 35   How Much Can You Spend to Generate an Enrollment?............................. 101
Chapter 36   Stepping Over Dollars to Pick-up Pennies.. 105
Chapter 37   "The Pulse of a School" 109
Chapter 38   Are You a Professional? 113
Chapter 39   How Does a Mile High Karate School Generate Revenue? 117
Chapter 40   HowI Opened Five schools in 18 Months with $10,000 when I was 23.... 121
Chapter 41   The Formula for Financial Success 125
Chapter 42   A$1,000,000.00 Watch and Other Tales of Entrepreneurship 129
Chapter 43   The Final Word...for Now... 133

Chapter 1

The Great Fallacies When You Start Your Business

Chapter 1

The Great Fallacies When You Start Your Business

When you first become self-employed there are often a series of fallacies that creep into your thinking without even being recognized or questioned. The following is far from an exhaustive set of these fallacies — but, clearly some of the major ones. To those of you who have been self-employed for some period of time — I apologize for belaboring what may appear obvious to you from your experience.

1: Now that you are self-employed you get to "set your own hours."

There's a joke. Once you become truly self-employed, the first indication may be that queasy feeling in the pit of your stomach that is your payroll, home payment and lease payment all coming due at the same time. My first time — to the best of my recall — was when suddenly I had $35,000+ due at the beginning of the month with about $4,000 on hand five days before. I dare you to put in your 40 hours when you are trying make payroll and insure that the lease is paid on time.

The reality, of course, is that as they transition from employee to business owner then to employer, most small business owners find that they go from a relatively fixed time schedule, guaranteed income and the ability to "turn-off" their work when they leave the office, to 100 hour weeks, getting paid last, if at all, and being mentally "on" 24 hours per day, seven days per week.

2: Adding employees means I have to do less myself.

A great quote, which I'm afraid I can't remember where I got it from, is "Always inspect what you expect. That's the way you get respect." Obviously, one person cannot do everything, and the only route to growth is adding additional people.

That being said, sometimes the added value of the person is outweighed by the amount of supervision required to insure that individual's productivity and contribution.

There are two truths of employees:

A. An owner will ALWAYS care more about the results than an employee.
B. Without aligned purposes and proper supervision — any employee (with rare exceptions) will ultimately detract from rather than add to the quality of your operation.

3: I'll build up my business then have an asset to sell.

Sorry about the wakeup call — but who are you going to sell it to? I've been approached to buy schools and seen desperate owners try to sell their businesses. You know the reality is you can only sell a karate school to a karate instructor — and that usually that means a Black Belt or employee in your school.

If you are lucky enough to find one with a "burning desire" and a huge nest egg, more power to you. More likely, when you decide to move on, you may be able to slowly turn the school over to an employee with a monthly payout. However don't be surprised if they can't run it as well as you do. And, what looked like a good deal for you changes rapidly when their finances are on the ropes and they are on the verge of eviction. I've accomplished this successfully, as have several of my friends — we'll review this more later — but it's really harder than it may seem to be at first.

4: The staff will run the show.

I'll just stop in and make the deposits and keep my own training high. First, see point #2 above, then realize that running a school profitably is difficult enough. A poorly-trained volunteer or poorly-paid staff is highly unlikely to keep things running at a level to support your lifestyle and to keep the school running at a high level. If they are running it really well, then their compensation and lifestyle better reflect their skill set pretty quickly, or they just may end up doing extremely well — across the street from you!

5: Now that I own the place...I'll teach the stuff that I enjoy.

Whoops — another reality check. The person who writes the checks is ultimately in charge. Wait: That's not you. The customer writes the check. Do what you enjoy and risk not finding anyone who wants to write the check. Ultimately, you must figure out what your market wants and give it to them. If you don't, someone else will. You just love the newest hard-core martial arts trend? Great — train to your heart's content on your own time, but be really careful not to skip giving your customers what they want.

6: I'm my own boss.

Interesting concept. Try explaining it to the IRS, your landlord, the city and county government, to the parents of your students, and, ultimately, to your many creditors and clients. As an employee, life is a little easier on a daily basis — you can look at your supervisor and take directions. As the owner, you have so many people trying to tell you what to do, that it's difficult to decide who to listen to first.

7: I can hire someone to "take care of the business side" of the school while I do the stuff I like — the teaching.

This one will get you in trouble in a big hurry. You'd better figure out every aspect of your school operation. Once you delegate an aspect, you still remain responsible.

As the owner you'd best develop a pretty good working knowledge of teaching, marketing, promotions, and advertising, sales, accounting, legal issues, staff hiring, staff training, human relations — and even basic repairs and maintenance.

Since you bought this program, I well understand that I am doing the proverbial "Preaching to the Choir."

But the reality is, that most martial arts school owners might really thrive working as instructors for someone else, unless they are really ready to do what YOU are already doing. Unless they are learning about marketing, understanding sales and really getting ready to be truly entrepreneurial, they really shouldn't be self-employed — they will never thrive as an independent business owner.

8: Once I've delegated a task– I don't have to worry about it anymore.

There are two different ways to hand off a task as the owner.
A. Delegation: Passing on responsibility for a task. Your role in this is to:
   1. Clearly define the task to be completely, with outcomes that define the successful completion;
   2. Provide training on key processes for the completion of the task.
   3. Involve the employee in defining the action plan for the accomplishment of the objective;
   4. Define benchmarks and timetables;
   5. Supervise at pre-defined intervals;
   6. Provide support and coaching during the process;

Quick Read: "Self Made In America," by John McCormick

7. Reward, train or punish for performance results.

Unfortunately, as the above implies, just because you have delegated a task and made an employee "responsible," does not mean that any of your own responsibility has been diminished.

Successful owners and managers are defined by their ability to train and support staff, and by their abilities to delegate tasks without losing track of the time-line or training needs.

B. Abdication: Handing off a task, then forgetting about it.

Many owners that I've met try this approach, especially with those tasks that they either don't understand or don't particularly enjoy.

Abdication of any IMPORTANT task is a sure and swift route to failure. Only you can be responsible for your success.

Chapter 2

The E-Myth

Chapter 2

The E-Myth

Years ago, at the recommendation of my friend Tom Callos, I read a book for which I have since gained increasing respect.

The book is called *The E-Myth* by a gentleman of the name of Michael Gerber. Since I first read his book, I've had several opportunities to hear him speak, and have met him in San Francisco. His book describes the martial arts "industry" perfectly.

He says that most small businesses in the United States were founded by a technician (read: Black Belt or Instructor), who one day had an "Entrepreneurial Seizure," and for some mysterious reason became convinced that they should be self-employed.

The ensuing reality is that the area that person was excellent in (in our industry, that is often martial athletics, or sometimes teaching) becomes a small part of their job. They now also have to understand and be good at marketing, sales, accounting, negotiations, legal issues and even facilities maintenance.

Most of these suddenly-independent business owners quickly find that they have to work a LOT harder than before for a substantially smaller amount of money, doing many activities for which they may, in fact, be poorly suited.

In fact, a majority of small businesses in the U.S. are "walking dead," struggling along with very little progress, working the owner into an early grave, and returning little in the way of financial rewards.

I don't think that it would be an exaggeration to say that martial arts school owners are often at the bottom of the heap when it comes to this pattern.

Quick Read: "The E-Myth," by Michael Gerber

Chapter 3

Wealth vs. Lifestyle

Chapter 3

Wealth vs. Lifestyle

Let's start with a few basic definitions:

Revenue or Gross Revenue: How much total cash comes through your business on a monthly, quarterly, or yearly basis.

Income or Net Income: How much you have available to you personally after ALL of the regular business expenses have been paid.

Wealth: How much in REAL assets you have accumulated. This includes: Equity in real estate, stocks and bonds, cash on hand and other truly valuable assets.

Lifestyle: The quality of your life now. This includes factors such as leisure time, travel, where you live, the quality of the furnishings, what you drive and how much real enjoyment you get our of life.

Now lets talk about reality. School owners love to brag about three things:

> **Number of students**
> **Size of their school**
> **Their GROSS revenue**

It's really interesting to watch. Get ten school owners together and watch them talk about themselves — and let the lying begin. *Student active counts* are the most exaggerated number of them all. With that being said, all of these numbers give you a small piece of the picture of their school and their business, but really none of them individually are of much interest to me.

Example 1: I have on close friend. His claim to fame was 1,000 students. But guess what? He was grossing in the range of $35,000 per month (scary huh?), and had a huge rent, payroll and other expense numbers. Many of these students were not really very solid — they just kind of came when they pleased and got rolled into the active

count for show. My friend worked 8 a.m.–10 p.m. daily and weekends, and had a huge renewal and retail push on Thanksgiving Day.

Example 2: Another friend told me he had 450 active. Most were kickboxing students on punch-cards. They attended sporadically, and as long as they came in at least monthly, they were considered an active student. He grossed about $7,500 per month in an 8,000-square-foot facility.

Example 3: I walked into a very small school owned by an acquaintance. Asked what the active count was — he said they had enrolled 1,400. When I asked for clarification, that turned out to be the number of enrollments that the school had done in the 12 years it had been open. I asked how many ACTIVE students they have, the owner replied that they had 450 students "on programs." Upon further questioning, I learned that meant anyone who's program had not expired (i.e.: I signed them to Black Belt three years ago; they paid in full; dropped out two months later; and have one year to go before their program "expires) counted. I then asked how many were actively attending. They had no idea!

Example 4: A very successful friend, with multiple schools and several locations grossing $35,000 to $40,000 each, and I compared financials. In five schools I grossed what he did in three, HOWEVER, my average rent was $2,700 — his was $6,500. My average school had two full-time employees and two part-time. His average school had five full-time employees. Well the bottom line was — my bottom line was really good. He had to put $45,000 into his operation to keep it operating smoothly.

Example 5: A friend runs a nice little, but somewhat mundane, operation. His gross is always

OKAY — not spectacular. His school only enrolls about eight new students per month, and his curriculum, frankly, bores me. However, he built his own building several years ago and started making double payments. He owns it outright now. That is: No rent, no mortgage payment and LOTS of equity. His nice little school runs at close to 50% net. Enough for a new Mercedes every couple of years, a few really nice vacations, and he really likes $300 shoes, so he buys them whenever he wants — and, don't forget the net-worth he has built!.

Don't let impressive numbers or an impressive facility fool you.

You know what I'd like to hear about?

1. What's the quality of your lifestyle? Do you enjoy life? Are you doing what you enjoy? Do you take time for hobbies, travel, family and entertainment? If you don't have time for these things because of your incredibly long hours, then, really, what good is the money? It's easy to get caught up in working and striving for more and more money, but money is only good for two things:

First, insuring that you can do and have the things you want RIGHT NOW. Are you able to afford those "toys" that are important to you? Do you refrain from spending money on things that won't contribute substantially to the quality of your life. Do you have expensive STUFF to impress others, or because you appreciate them personally?

Second, so that you can build security for your future — and I don't necessarily just mean for your retirement. What if your school has a down-turn (remember all kinds of unexpected things can happen)? Are you financially strong enough to weather the storm? What if one of your kids has unexpected medical expenses, or if you have a medical emergency?

2. What's your NET Income? How much money do you have left over from your business after EVERYONE ELSE gets paid? If your expenses are in line and your gross is adequate or excellent, you could have 15%, 25% or maybe even 45% or 50% left over. Do $30,000 per month with $15,000 left over, and I'll think you are incredible. Do $180,000 per month with $3,000 left over — well nothing personal, but who cares?

3. How much Net Worth have you built, and how much do you save? Do you have equity in your home? Equity in the building that houses your school? How's your IRA, savings, and investments? Does your SCHWAB account grow every month, or are you living week to week? Forget about the guy who boasts a huge student base — I want to be like a friend of mine who bought the building that houses his school, and ended up owning the whole city block, with positive cash-flow from rental income and huge equity. Not very glamorous in the "bragging rights" pool at the next karate tournament or business convention, but hey, he paid HIMSELF first!

4. How much have you learned this week, month and year? If you are constantly learning, you will always be about to recover from setbacks as well as capitalize on new opportunities.

Stuff: Your day-to-day lifestyle expenses must really be determined by what is really going to add enjoyment to your life, relative to the costs.

A Personal Example

Many years ago, many friends and employees laughed at me (remember when they laugh, it's your money not theirs). Why did they laugh? Well, once a year, I would hold a Christmas party at my house — which is huge, beautiful, in one of the most expensive neighborhoods in the Denver metro area and has tremendous views overlooking the city. At the same time, on a day-to-day basis, I drove an Audi 4000, which was at about 150,000 miles (I finally traded it when it failed the emissions inspection, got damaged by hail and needed more repairs than it was worth). During this period, my house appreciated over $300,000, and my car basically went from the $20,000 I paid for it new to a value of $0.

Often, we are tempted to buy things based upon the image we hope to project to friends, neighbors, business associates and others.

If you really want that expensive toy because it enhances your enjoyment on a day-by-day basis, then by all means, get it and enjoy it. Just decide, on a daily basis, not because of the "image" you hope to project, or because of an attempt to impress your friends.

Remember, about the only thing that you can buy for yourself that has any real value after you buy it is your home.

Everything else, with very few exceptions, begins to depreciate or have minimal value right after you've spent the money.

Cars: NEVER buy one new. Guess what happens–the minute you drive it off the lot? It loses at least 20 to 25% of it's value. Want to have fun with your car? What's the difference between brand new and a couple of years old, and 10,000–20,000 or even 30,000 miles? I'll tell you the difference on a Jaguar I bought recently: about $20,000!

Furniture: Just try selling that $2,000 or $3,000 sofa or table. Guess what? You might just be able to get 10% of what you paid.

Art and Jewelry: People fool themselves into thinking that these items have value. Certainly if you are a serious investor, if you buy at wholesale and have access to quality channels of resale, then you might come out okay on some of these things. The reality is, almost any ring, watch or painting you buy is going to immediately have close to zero value.

Electronics, computers, stereos, etc.: Here again, buy what you will truly enjoy, but plan on these items having no value once you have purchased them.

When you start reviewing your assets and computing your net worth, your real estate, stocks, bonds and other assets have real investment value. Home furnishings, art and jewelry probably have only utilitarian or sentimental value once you've left the store. Cars begin to depreciate the minute you drive off the lot. Remember this when deciding on that new luxury car or whether to invest in a nicer home.

A book that should be required reading is *The Millionaire Next Door*. This book teaches some great lessons in wealth accumulation.

Quick Read: "The Millionaire Next Door", by Dr. Thomas Stanley

Quick Read: "Financial Self-Defense," by Charles Givens

Chapter 4

First Figure Out What You LOVE

Chapter 4

First Figure Out What You LOVE

I really think that rule number one in deciding what you are going to do and how your business is going to unfold, is to figure out what you really love to do.

If you really love to teach on a daily basis, then you probably never want to open multiple locations.

If you really enjoy training, you may want to consider something else as a career, then slot your leisure time for your martial arts training.

I've seen many schools begin because a Black Belt just really loved to compete or to train. That's a bad basis for beginning a school that requires teaching, marketing, accounting and a host of other skills and time commitments.

Quick Read: "Peak Performers," by Charles Garfield

Chapter 5

Everything is Negotiable

Chapter 5

Everything is Negotiable

Just assume that anything that you need to buy, paying a monthly payment on or owe is negotiable.

Clearly, some things are more difficult to negotiate than others, but ultimately, just about anything can be negotiated.

Example: Did you sign a five- or ten-year lease when you opened — perhaps with stars in your eyes? It looked like the greatest thing ever. Suddenly a couple of years later, the payment begins to look like the national debt.

Well, start by taking a look at your situation from the other side of the table.

Does your owner have a full center and a waiting list to get in at 20% more than you are paying? In that case, it might be real easy to sublet, or just be excused from your lease, so that the owner can shift to a "more substantial" client with an even higher lease payment.

If you were in that owner's place, wouldn't you be in a huge hurry to release a tenant at a lower rate and then re-lease to a higher paying tenant ,and possibly even to a national credit tenant?

Discuss the situation with the owner or a realtor. Look for alternative space that is either smaller or leases at a lower amount per foot, or both. Sometimes it's also possible to move within the same center to a smaller space, or to a less desirable space. Either way, this lowers your monthly outlay.

Or, are you really about the only substantial tenant in a shopping center that looks like it's about to be condemned? That's a perfect opportunity to renegotiate your lease. Why? Well, what happens if you go out of business or just walk on the lease? First, the owner has to go looking for another tenant. If he already has vacancies, he's been doing that without a lot of luck already hasn't he? Once he finds a new tenant then he has to pay realtor a commission, possibly pay for tenant finish, maybe provide some free rent, and definitely wait another two to six months to start collecting rents until the new tenant opens.

You may have to be pretty tough in the negotiations in this case. Your owner may already be operating on a negative cash basis. You really have to make sure he believes that you are either:

A. On the brink of insolvency, or that without a break, you won't stay in business much longer, or;

B. That you are ready to "walk away" from the lease and that you are really unconcerned about his possible legal remedies.

Both of these examples are obviously extreme, but they give you the idea. If you want to pay your landlord $500 less per month for three years, that adds up to $18,000. What's it going to cost him to re-lease the space. Figure out the downtime, realtor fees, tenant finish and free rent the owner will have to incur. Also, figure out what your real market rental should be — if you are paying over the market that's a negotiating point in your favor. But, it would be one reason the owner may fight to keep you in your lease rather than putting the space on the market.

As an aside: You are much better off in dealing with your lease if you are NOT personally signed on the lease, and don't have a lot of assets in the corporation that runs your school. More on this later.

Another example: Let's say you spent $10,000 with your local television station, radio station or newspaper. The ads ran — and not too unusually, the phones didn't ring. Rather than the flood of calls you expected, you get four calls and two enrollments. Then the bill shows up. What do you do?

Well you can do several things:

- Just pay the bill, take your lumps and walk away;
- Sit down with the ad rep, his supervisor and anyone else you can get in front of, and explain you dilemma. Explain that $25 per call would be great. $50 per call, okay, Maybe you could even live with $100 per call.
- Offer to either pay your maximum: $50 per call on what you've already run, or;
- Explain that you'd be happy if they kept running the commercials. They can even tweak the ad and the run times until you are up to 100 to 200 calls (walk them through what you will do to keep excellent track of the results).

If they refuse the options above either:

- Send them the check for $100 per call with an endorsement that spells out that in depositing the check, the invoice amount is paid in full;
- Put the bill in your drawer. Six or eight months later when their collections people call, explain the situation and offer to settle for the amount previously offered.

Example Number Three: The sales rep for your local newspaper shows up and practically guarantees that the ads in his/her newspaper will be the greatest thing ever for your business.

- Explain to the sales rep that if what he explains turns out to be true, then you'll both be overjoyed — but ask what guarantee do they offer?
- Explain that you are willing to pay $50 per call — no more.

You may be able to negotiate one of several things:

First: To pay per-inquiry, rather than just buying space.

Second: An agreement for "make goods" free of charge if the initial run does not get the needed response.

At the very least, you have established your negotiating position properly when the bill comes due.

Chapter 6

Fire Those Who "Suck the Life" from Your School

Chapter 6

Fire Those Who "Suck the Life" from Your School

I was listening to Tom Peters one day and he was talking about an accounting firm that took a rather radical approach to building their business: they fired the bottom 30% of their clients!

They sat down, took a look a their client roster, and evaluated them on the basis of several factors:

- Is this someone that we enjoy working with, who adds value to our practice and who enhances our business?
- Is this someone who pays on time and contributes at a level proportionate to the time they take to service.

I really hate to admit it, but I used this idea rather aggressively a few years back, and gee, it really worked.

How did I go about this?

Well, I had a branch that had been doing extremely poorly. Things just really hadn't been run properly. Unfortunately, my staff really enjoyed working out, but didn't care much for marketing, or even for paying attention to student retention.

When I personally took over the location, there were major problems, to say the least. Radical changes upset many (if you can say many with the tiny active count they had accrued). As usual, the major problems come from the Black Belts, followed by the Brown Belts.

Maybe I was just in a bad mood, but I basically made radical changes. When senior students complained, I explained as nicely as possible that it was my way or the highway. They would either adjust and be supportive, or find some other place to be happy.

Sure enough, I irritated or just plain fired about 24 people. Then guess what? The school got to be a lot more fun. The negative undercurrents disappeared, and the school went from 95 to 310 students in about 12 months! The really loyal Black Belts chipped in and suddenly became strong leaders when space was made for them, and the negative energy was erased.

I was speaking to a very well-known industry leader several years ago while holding a seminar for and teaching his staff and associates. He actually suggested that he wanted to eliminate the parent seating area in his school to "keep the parents from sitting there bitching about things the entire class."

One way you could evaluate this comment is that there must be a really mediocre level of student service overall in that school, if the complaining parents were prevalent enough to actually consider eliminating the seating area.

However, I'd be the first to admit that no matter how good you are, there's always that bottom 5% who, no matter what you do, are going to be negative — and a certain group for whom your philosophies and theirs are just never going to completely align.

You may be far better off to address the bitching/moaning crowd head-on whenever possible, one on one, never in groups.

Before you do, take an OBJECTIVE look at what's going on. You might find they are RIGHT. If you've dropped the ball on service with this family, generally been sloppy in your follow-through, or just haven't performed at your peak, then by all means, admit it, fix it, regain trust and create a friend. Those who complain — if treated properly and paid attention to at the right time — can become your most loyal students.

After following the above steps and taking an objective look at things, there may just be some parents and students that would be better off somewhere else. Additionally, life is just too short to deal with some people. When you've decided to fire a student, do it nicely and hit things head on.

Take all of the blame. Explain that you have obviously not met their families' expectations. You really don't want to continue to disappoint their family and are sure that there are other schools or other activities that they will enjoy considerably more than your school.

As a side note: After terminating several families, they ended up at the school of someone I just didn't like very well. You know what — it really was the best of all worlds to imagine him having to deal with all of the irritations that I had put up with for so long. Sometime there's just not enough money in the world…

Not to get too mercenary, but the same concept applies to your staff as well. Once you end up with a substantial number of people on your payroll, you'll start to notice an interesting phenomenon. Any time that you and your senior people or senior person (or maybe it's you and your wife or husband) discuss your staff problems, needs and concerns, one or two people consume the vast majority of the conversations.

With 40–50 staff members, I always found that our management team continually had problems with 3 to 5 people. They were the focal point of almost all of the problems.

An adjunct to this is that I've found that as soon as you've started thinking about firing someone, it's probably already been too long.

It's important to be fair, and not to act in such a way to make your staff insecure. However, consider two things:

• Would your life improve if you terminated your bottom 2, 3 or 5 employees?
• Do you have someone who has been a big problem you've avoided dealing with? It's easiest to NOT deal with a problem until it has grown and festered out of control. Address problem people head-on.

• Do you have someone working for you with a bad attitude?
• Do you have someone who just drains your energy?

Nick Cokinos has a great saying that applies here:

"I'd rather have a crisis than a sloppy situation."

Keep in mind, that any sloppy situation becomes a crisis — sometimes an unrecoverable crisis — on it's own schedule. Become pro-active. Hit problems head-on. And your life, and income, will improve immeasurably.

Quick Read: "A Passion for Excellence," by Peters and Austin.

Quick Read: "The Pursuit of WOW!," by Tom Peters.

Chapter 7

Separate Your Hobby from Your Business

Chapter 7

Separate Your Hobby from Your Business

Most school owners end up running a school, as their hobby gradually evolves into a job, then into a career. Maybe they were recruited to teach by their instructor, then had their "entrepreneurial seizure" and ended up self-employed.

This is, of course, considerably different from the more pedestrian career path of most professionals: complete high school; go to college to pursue a degree in a field expected to produce an interesting and lucrative career; find the job and pursue career advancement and consistently improving salary and benefits. Certainly in the new economy that model is becoming increasingly less common. However, I walk through this to point out how different our industry usually is.

Although there is a newer generation, many like myself actually trained to improve their teaching skill, pursued a degree in business and additional training in marketing, and really approached the martial arts as a career. Generally that's the exception in the martial arts.

If you are really interested in running a quality school and making a reasonable income, then you must approach your business as a career, and not as a way to pursue your hobby full-time.

I've always held myself to a standard of matching my income opportunities in any other pursuit by plus or minus 10%. I've always planned on consistently matching my other choices.

A quick lesson in economics versus accounting:

If your revenue exceeds your expenses, you will end up with what your accountant calls *net profit*. Although certainly having a positive bottom line is a good thing, it misses an important component:

Opportunity Cost

Opportunity cost is, in simple terms, what you could have made doing something else.

Example: If you could earn $50,000 per year in some other career, and you make $40,000 running your school, your accountant will tell you that you made $40,000 profit; but an economist would tell you that you lost $10,000 compared to your other opportunities. If you made $50,000 from the school, then actually you have broken even compared to your other opportunities.

The next issue to always pay attention to is your classroom and curriculum:

Do you teach what you like or teach what your clients want to learn?

Many, many martial artists pursue their own interests and hobbies in martial arts — then immediately convert their curriculum into these areas.

Example: The ultimate fighting challenge takes the martial arts community by storm. School owners around the country take up grappling and pursue any of the Gracie clan or Machado family to teach them this kick-ass Brazilian martial art. Convinced that this was the ultimate fighting method, and enamored of the viciousness of the telecasts, they immediately begin teaching grappling classes on a regular basis and expose their entire student body to this new curriculum.

Ultimately, the moderately successful school, that previously had a solid children's and family clientele, erodes. The owner has great fun with this new curriculum, but the students don't share his new-found interest. The owner convinces himself that the kids and parents just love this new curriculum, yet his active count slowly dwindles.

Do You Just Love Tournaments?

Is that the best thing for your students? I've run one of the biggest tournaments in the country, but I've got to tell you that I've never seen open tournaments have a positive impact on a school or on a student.

Do You Just Love to Train with Knives?

Not a great way to impress the parents is it?

Keep in mind that your personal hobbies in the martial arts and your career running a school should be kept separate. That doesn't mean that you shouldn't pursue those things that you enjoy. Just step back and objectively evaluate whether what turns you on is the same thing that your clients and prospective clients are looking for when they come to your school.

Chapter 8

*Manage Your Time,
Live Your Life*

Chapter 8

Manage Your Time, Live Your Life

In a martial arts school operation, there are two major time-management problems that school owners encounter for themselves:

First: Deciding that their work day is from 5 p.m. to 9 p.m., then spending their day with a variety of time-wasting activities. The reality of a school is that there are lots of important activities that should be accomplished during non-prime time hours.

Remember that during class hours if you are not teaching or personally interacting with students and parents, then you are misusing your time. These are typically the only hours where you can really communicate with your students.

What do you do during non-class hours?

Almost all external promotional and marketing activities, including:

- Meeting with local elementary schools;
- Meeting with local merchants to line-up co-promotional opportunities;
- Exploring advertising and marketing opportunities;
- Writing up marketing letters for your old prospects;
- Organizing your exam list and reviewing attendance records of your students;
- Reviewing your inactive student list–and making a plan for their reactivation;
- Updating your computer system and keeping your stats up to date.

The main issue is that you must distinguish between prime-time activities and non-prime time activities. All administrative duties should be accomplished only during non-prime time hours.

Second: Failing to manage time effectively on an hour-by-hour basis and minute-by-minute basis.

How do you manage your time effectively?

1. Use an effective planning system. I prefer Franklin Planners. They are more expensive than some of the other systems, but given the value of the addition to your life, it is well worth the expense.

   When using the Franklin system, I really end up planning on a quarterly and monthly basis for many activities — more so than really focusing on every quarter hour.

   During the evening as long as you keep your objectives clear; it can be relatively easy to manage your evening hours;

2. Use an adequate school management software system to keep your intro appointments and your prospects under control. Currently, there are several fine systems on the market. Naturally, I prefer the system that I designed from the ground up, Master Vision. However, I would be the first to admit that other systems have similar capabilities to allow you to organize your day effectively.

3. Prioritize appropriately. I highly recommend that you read *First Things First* by Steven Covey, or, at least, study this chapter in *7-Habits of Highly Effective People*.

To summarize Covey's concepts, all activities fall into one of four quadrants:

1. Urgent and Important
2. Not Urgent and Important
3. Urgent and Not Important
4. Not Urgent and Not Important

A karate school in prime-time (i.e.: 4 p.m. to 8 p.m.) is full of quadrant 1 and quadrant 3 activities. On a minute-by-minute basis, the evening is full of ringing telephones, constant questions, classes that must begin and end on time, and the constant parade of important and unimportant urgencies.

During your evening to be effective remember there are really only three important elements:

Enrollments
Retention
Renewals

If an activity does not positively contribute to one of these then it falls into the "Not Important" category.

What mediocre school operators fail to focus on are that those are important areas, but not urgent.

Generally important but not urgent areas include:
- Internal and external marketing efforts;
- Student retention;
- Renewal preparation.

A note about students and your time:

With few exceptions, your time can be eaten up by students who fit in one of two categories.

1. Your AAA Black Belt Club, 5-days-per-week loyalists and your D-negative and disgruntled students.

    You must be careful not to devote too much prime time to students in either of these categories.

2. Your AAA students will spend time talking and in your presence just because they really can't get enough of you and your school.

    Your D-negative students often have a negative outlook in all areas of their life and just want to complain to anyone who will listen. In any conversation of this type, work on keeping the conversation short and on subject.

A few ways to accomplish this is: don't sit down, don't go in your office — address the issues at hand quickly and directly, suggest scheduling a specific appointment time when it's appropriate for your time availability.

Third: By spending excess time on "hobby" martial arts activities while rationalizing that you are really working on the school.

Fourth: Failing to structure your day effectively.

To structure your day effectively, it's important to figure out how you personally function best, and then plan your activities around your own peak times of efficiency.

A few years ago there seemed to be this myth that successful school owners rose at dawn and were in their office by 8:00 am.

This works real well for some of my closest friends, but, for me, this has always been massively counter-productive.

All martial arts school operators must be at their absolute peak between the hours of 4 p.m. and 8 p.m. You must figure out when your creative hours are for planning and development, and also structure your days to hit your peak during prime-time hours.

For myself, I am mostly creative late at night. At the time when most of my friends are climbing into bed, I am just getting going. Most of this book was written between 11 p.m. and 3 a.m. I like to get going mid-morning, take a break mid-day, and then hit school operations hard during prime time. Depending upon what I need to accomplish, I will either take a break and go to a movie, or grab a quick bite to eat and then work on my creative projects, either writing lesson plans, designing ad campaigns and writing.

Quick Read: "First Things First,"
by Steven Covey

Quick Read: "The One Minute Manager Meets the Monkey,"
by Blanchard/Oncken

Quick Read: "Managing Management Time,"
by William Oncken

For best time management, you can get a lot more work done when no one is around to interrupt, and when the phones aren't ringing. If you are an early-bird, 5 or 6 a.m. might be best for you. Again, for me, anything creative gets accomplished after 11 p.m. If I return your e-mail, it may be at 2 or 3 a.m.

Chapter 9

Bigger Isn't Always Better

Chapter 9

Bigger Isn't Always Better

When I was younger, I was often envious of friends and acquaintances, and even instructors that I had heard about who:

- Boasted larger student active counts than my own.
- Had huge, beautiful facilities;
- Who's gross was touted to be larger than mine.

Over the years, having been there and done that at every level, I've started to realize what never really came to mind in my younger days:

Happiness on a daily basis is really more important than all of those ego-building, but often misleading, measures of success.

Your net is way more important than your gross. In fact, your gross is only important RELATIVE to your expense structure.

Your facility should do two things:

1. Present a positive first impression to prospective students and provide a quality, learning environment to your current students.
2. Have adequate space to safely and efficiently teach your existing active count, taking into account maximizing your space utilization through proper scheduling, etc.

Everything else is EGO.

Lifestyle counts! Work 100 hours a week for $200,000, or 40 hours per week and make $100,000 — which really enhances your life more?

Wait a minute! If I had hobbies, what would they be?

- Did I miss the kids growing up?
- Do I take time to learn and grow?
- How about relaxation and recharge time?

Wealth — live below your means. Make intelligent decisions so as to accumulate assets. Long-term security is based upon REAL assets, like real estate, bonds, publicly traded stocks (including mutual and index funds) and your bank balance. Balance your current lifestyle expenses with building for the future.

Impress your clients — your students and parents — not your competitors and peers. Let's face it: Why do you care what the other martial arts guys think?

Chapter 10

Networking Your Way to Everything You Need to Know

Chapter 10

Networking Your Way to Everything
You Need to Know

The statement that is propagated by those who externalize their successes (or failures) is, "It's not what you know — it's who you know." Often, the tone and implication is that those who've succeeded were just born lucky or connected. Their family or pre-school class was just unnaturally well-connected to the "right people." The implication is that since you were not BORN with the same connections, there's just no hope to have comparable success.

Not to burst their bubble, but in the vast majority of cases, those who have made the right connections are those who made friends, learned about people, served without expectation of a immediate or even direct return, and made a concerted effort to build and maintain friendships.

How do you network and build positive relationships effectively?

First: This is really important — Really be a QUALITY person. What's that mean in this context?

Well the short list is:

Be a student. We're not talking about formal academics here. READ. Read a lot. Read about subjects that you are interest in learning more about. Read about things that you really need to understand to be successful.

You will gain more respect if you can hold an intelligent conversation on the topics at hand. If you have a solid knowledge base, you are certainly perceived to be intelligent and a valuable contributor.

Be FOCUSED and goal oriented.

We've all read about how to set goals.

SMART Goals (Specific, Measurable, Attainable, Realistic, and Tangible.)

You already know this from watching your students. However, you may not recognize it in yourself. Goal-oriented people exude a focus, confidence and self discipline that attracts other success-oriented people.

Be interested in people. Ask questions. Get them talking about themselves. Remember the details THAT ARE IMPORTANT to them.

Learn to SHUT UP. Talking about yourself beyond a foundational background to establish credibility puts people to sleep. People love to talk about themselves.

Project a successful image that is in-sync with the key leaders in any environment.

Second Isolate those people who can add value to your life.

In any crowd, figure out who could teach you something or add real value to your life is some way. This is difficult to pre-judge, but isolate a few individuals whom you want to meet. Many people think that networking at a seminar means meeting everyone and exchanging lots of business cards — soon to be discarded. I'd rather leave with one or two new friends and then meet their friends and acquaintances.

Third: Find a way to add value.

Any high profile leader, speaker, consultant or business operator is inundated with people who all want something from them. They have secretaries, assistants, and even bodyguards, whose sole function is to guard them from self-centered masses who want something for nothing from them, who waste their time, and distract them from their real objectives.

Figure out what the other person values, and what they are really passionate about. Wherever you have the ability, find a way enhance areas that they care about passionately.

Fourth: Give without expectation of a payback.

Go above and beyond with those whom you decide to network. If you give without immediate expectation of payback, your contributions will be perceived as sincere, because they *are* sincere.

Fifth: Choose seminars and other events as much for who is attending as for who is speaking. There are some events where the only real valuable contact is the keynote speaker who's speaking to 2,500 people. That's tough. Another one had 75 high-quality people attending with several quality presenters and provided much more likelihood of leaving with a few new peers or mentors who can add value.

Sixth: Be unique. Without unnecessary flamboyance, have a few unique traits that are memorable in a positive way.

Seventh: Follow-up. Go to "Successories," some other quality card shop, or print up some custom note cards. When you meet someone new, drop them a note. Doesn't have to be anything fancy, just "nice meeting you," or "thank you for your contribution," etc.

Make notes to yourself about their interests and needs. When you come across an article, book, or contact that might be valuable then mail it or call them with this information or contact.

Eight: Be too busy to be a pest. If you are goal oriented and focused, you are highly unlikely to waste anyone's time. Be respectful of people's time. Call with a specific question or a specific contribution. Don't waste anyone's time.

Nine: Don't be a FAN or groupie. Although momentarily flattering, no one really wants to spend time with dreamy-eyed fans. You and I want to spend time talking to people who can contribute to and support our own objectives, not just those who seek autographs, pictures, or association with fame.

Ten: Don't be afraid to approach the "big fish." They are just people, too, and may be hungry for someone to just talk to them as a person.

Quick Read: "Networking with the Affluent," by Dr. Thomas Stanley

Quick Read: "How to Win Friends and Influence People," and "Dig Your Well Before You're Thirsty" by Harvey McCay

A couple of personal case studies:

Chuck Norris and the *Side Kicks* Tour. In 1987 and 1988 I first started exploring the idea of promoting a national karate tournament. Soon after being accepted as a NASKA national promoter, I began to get acquainted with the other promoters. It was clear that some would do little to enhance my life; however the real leaders all had value to add and some real qualities. Gradually, using many of the steps outline above, I moved

into the "inner circle," networking with Larry Carnahan, Joe Corley, Rich Baptista, and Mike McCoy and his partner Mike Sawyer.

On the circuit, this often ended up with a small group having a nice dinner in whatever town we were visiting, or my dragging a small group to a movie, the beach or some other interesting excursion.

After a couple of years I ended up at the U.S. Open in Orlando, promoted by close friends (who I had never met before becoming a promoter) Mike Sawyer and Mike McCoy. After the even I invited myself along to an intimate dinner with Mike Sawyer, Larry Carnahan, Mike McCoy, Chuck Norris and a couple of people that I had never met before. While everyone else focused

on Chuck, I began talking the quiet and really pleasant couple sitting with me at the end of the table. It turned out they were Jim and Linda MacInvale.

He turned out to be "Mattress Mac," a well-known Houston entrepreneur of Gallery Furniture (and Gallery Films). This rather shy, non-descript, and certainly rather shabbily-dressed man had personally financed the movie *Side Kicks* to the tune of about $8 million at that point. We had a pleasant conversation, exchanged business cards and talked briefly about common interests.

Of course, after dinner we all did the requisite photos with Chuck Norris and said goodnight. On Monday I got my cards out and sent a follow-up note to Jim and Linda: "Great to meet you in Denver. Was fascinated to hear about your business. Would love to come to Houston sometime and learn from your operation. Thanks, Steve."

I don't remember if I even left knowing how to get hold of Chuck Norris. If so, I'm sure I dropped him a note as well. It was quite a while later, at least a year, that I learned from Mike Sawyer that *Side Kicks* had been released, and that Chuck was hoping to get karate schools promoting the movie.

When I heard that I asked how I could help, and then did 500%.

I got copies of their promo videotape. I sent copies to friends that I knew had cable TV shows, who immediately put them on the air (John Graden, Tom Callos, and others). I started showing the promo reel to my students. I called Mike Sawyer and brainstormed on ways that I could help, and that the industry, in general, could help. Then called Jim McInvale to ask how I could help them in their promotions.

Note: This was all with no real expected payback other than if *Side Kicks* became the next *Karate Kid* I figured it would be good for business.

Then after the second or third call to Jim to give ideas and connect him to friends in the industry, he mentioned that Chuck Norris was doing a national tour to support the movie. When I found out he was visiting Denver, I immediately started looking for ways to help support their tour in Denver. After lots of contribution, I talked to Jim about having a visit to my school. The basic response was: "Mr. Norris's policy on this tour is not to visit ANY karate schools, however, you have

Quick Read: "Behind the Golden Arches," by John Love

Quick Read: "Grinding it Out," by Ray Kroc

been such a huge help I'm sure we can make an exception."

After our confirmation of the schedule for his visit in Denver I tripled my effort to help promote *Side Kicks* and I mean really went above and beyond. We faxed letters and made calls to every school in town inviting the kids to come and meet Chuck Norris, talked to all of the theaters to ask how we could help, contacted every radio station, TV station and newspaper. And offered to split the cost of ads in the major papers promoting the personal appearances at the theaters and at the karate schools. We also talked with the theaters about offering free month passes to everyone who bought a ticket to *Side Kicks*.

Actually, Chuck tried to back out of visiting my school after we had already promoted it because of his "No Karate Schools" policy. Jim nicely explained to him that NOBODY had done as much to support their effort and they absolutely had to return the favor.

Quick Read: "Dig Your Well Before You Are Thirsty," by Harvey McCay.

In fact, our first face-to-face interaction in Denver was with a beta-cam in my face and Chuck saying, "Steve, I'm sorry. I know you're pissed, but get over it. You are on Entertainment Tonight (and, in fact the visit to the school was featured on the show).

Well, we had so many people at the karate school, that we literally ended up with 15 police officers directing traffic and a line around the building. We did TV interviews with all of the major affiliate stations in my office, with a Mile High Karate banner in back, and in most of the stories they started with exterior shots of our sign and of the crowds. A few weeks later, I ended up meeting Chuck Norris with Bob Wall and Mike Sawyer at Chuck Norris's ranch in Navasota to discuss other potential business opportunities to work together.

Shortly thereafter, I introduced Chuck Norris to the EFC Board of Directors and to Nick Cokinos. While at his ranch, I got autographed pictures for all of the movie theater district managers and personally mailed or delivered them with a "Thank You" note from me for their help during the visit of my friend.

That eventually led to a series of ads featuring Chuck Norris that I developed for use by EFC schools, and fundraising efforts by my schools of over $50,000 to his Kick Drugs Foundation, and over $500,000 raised through EFC schools. For three or four years, I was always his official host at our annual EFC Conventions.

I've continued to help in fundraising for Kick Drugs Out of America. Now, this is important: I do it because I believe in their cause and I truly like the people involved and want to help, NOT with any expected return. Also, I've had the privilege of being able to contribute ideas regarding instructor recruitment and training with their head instructor, Ed Saenz. Oh, and I got to hang out on the set of *Walker, Texas Ranger*, be technical director for a karate tournament they filmed, and a center referee for the climatic fight scene. I don't think I'll be taking over Chuck Norris's spot, but it was a lot of fun.

Remember: Meet people who can contribute. Make a contribution. Be unique. Don't waste their time. Follow-up.

A couple of quick thoughts: Be memorable for SOMETHING. I am often memorable because I read so much. Often when a topic that I have a passing familiarity with comes up, I've often read several books on the subject.

Therefore, when I find out what someone is interested in, I will often talk to them about the topic a little, find out if they've read one of my favorite books, and if not, send them the book. This accomplishes several things simultaneously:

- Anchors a memorable trait that I have in their mind.
- Adds value for them on a subject that they have expressed an interest in already.
- Gives a follow-up to our conversation in a way that reinforces that I remembered their interests.

Amazon.com is a wonderful way to expedite your follow-up. You can order on-line, complete the card and have whatever book drop shipped right away.

Keep note-cards on hand. I even keep them in my day planner and have even been known to address follow-up cards to people I meet in a meeting while I'm still sitting in the meeting or seminar.

Always figure out WHO you should meet at any gathering. Make an effort to meet them, create conversation and find common interests.

Example: At a recent internet marketing seminar that I attended, which was all day Friday, Saturday and Sunday, I approached the host/promoter with whom I already had a pretty good relationship and asked, "Who is there here that I MUST meet before this is over?" He went through a list of about 10 people, 6 of whom I had already met and 4 of whom I was unaware of. Sure enough, he introduced me and gave them a couple of reasons to be interested in meeting me. Mission accomplished. It was now important for me to follow the process discussed already to maintain contact.

These three books make up the ultimate collection of networking ideas and implementation steps available. If you want to have access to the best and the brightest then you really must devour these books and act on the content.

Chapter 11
Always Protect Yourself First

Chapter 11

Always Protect Yourself First

Positive thinking is a wonderful thing. No one ever accomplished much with a defeatist attitude or with low expectations for themselves and those around them. All great entrepreneurial success comes first from a vision based upon possibilities.

However, in the real world, most great successes have been accomplished by intermediate failures. I suggest that you read biographies of great entrepreneurial successes. My favorites tell the story of Tom Monahan of Dominos Pizza fame and the story of Ray Kroc or McDonald's fame.

Perhaps a better way to address this is to expect the best and prepare for the worst. Early on in your business and at all stages, always put everything in place to insolate yourself from the worst case scenario.

Action steps:

- NEVER sign personally on any lease. Although every landlord will insist that you give a personal guarantee, don't do it. Be prepared to walk away from the lease negotiations if the owner will not agree to this condition.
- Always operate your school as a CORPORATION not as an individual proprietorship or as a partnership.
- Keep everything in place to avoid "Piercing the Corporate Veil:"

- Keep your funds separate. At the very least, maintain a personal and a corporate checking account. Do not intermingle funds. Pay corporate expenses out of your corporate account and personal expenses out of your business account.
- Maintain all required corporate paperwork up to date.
- Operate at all times as a corporation. Don't blur the lines between you as the Master Instructor and your corporation as the operator of your school.
- Maintain adequate school liability insurance at all times.
- Maintain workman's compensation insurance at all times.
- Pay yourself a monthly salary and, always cut the check.

A great read is about an orphan who starts a pizza restaurant by the University of Michigan campus that becomes Dominos Pizza. During his growth trend, he went broke about four times. He once had the warehouse burn down with no insurance. At another time, he had the IRS walking into stores carting out ovens and typewriters for back taxes. Not exactly the "born with a silver spoon" expected success story. During the process he built the #1 Pizza Delivery business in the world while amassing a huge success literature library. A really inspirational read for anyone who feels like they keep fighting the odds or who has experienced any level of financial crisis.

Ray Kroc is another really interesting success story. He was in his 50's, when as a mixmaster salesperson, he was tuned in to notice something really strange: A little hamburger stand in California was using more of his machines then 6, or even 10, other similar restaurants.

When he went to investigate, he found a thriving operation being run by the McDonald brothers. He immediately negotiated rights to franchise the concept, and off he ran into one huge wall after another. In the early stages, he was unable to gain cooperation from the McDonald brothers and had his hands tied, unable to make necessary decisions — some even as basic as modifying the restaurant design to allow for heating needs when building stores in Illinois. He repeatedly ran out of money and ran into incredible obstacles, yet miraculously built the largest restaurant chain in the world to become the second largest property owner in the world, right behind the Catholic church.

Chapter 12

*Things are Never as Bad
as You Think They Are*

Chapter 12

Things are Never as Bad as You Think They Are

No business owner has ever lasted for long without some really bad days. Life is full of disappointments and stress factors. Just expect that they are part of the process and learn to cope.

At *Date with Destiny* with Tony Robbins, he talked about how one criteria for being successful financially was the ability to cope with financial stress. He discussed that for his business that he had to come up with a little over a million dollars in the next week, and wasn't quite sure where it was going to come from.

In the normal course of running your business you can decide to stay small and grow slowly, if at all, or you can take increasingly bigger risks and have larger and larger financial commitments and decisions.

An important skill to learn is to cope with stress — the stress that comes with financial stress and with the day-to-day disappointments that can come with running your business.

The best way to cope with these stressors is to learn to step back and view your situation objectively. Learn to emotionally and physically step outside of your situation and look at what's really going on around you. In the midst of real or perceived crisis, if you stay in a subjective and emotional state, surrounded by the problem or problems, then your reaction often will be panic, possibly eventually even numbness and inactivity.

The way out of a crisis is to follow the following steps:

1. Step out of the situation, mentally and physically.
2. Look at what's happening to you as objectively as possible — as if it is happening to someone else and not to you.

3. Think about what advice you would give to someone else if they were in this situation.

Focus on where you want to be, not where you are. Focus on your desired outcome, not on your current problem.

Ask effective questions:

If I were to accomplish_____how would I do it? Not, why is this happening to me? *In order to solve _____ what would I do next?*

Ask yourself: *What's the worst that could happen? Could I live with that?* Even the worst is rarely as bad as your emotionally reaction makes it seem.

TAKE ACTION! Fear tends to immobilize. If you aggressively take action to move things back in the direction that you want them to take, you will become more confident, motivated, and successful.

Remember this: Even if you do not know what to do next, DO SOMETHING! The act of taking bold and aggressive action will mold your emotional state to be more resourceful and more effective.

You can learn to create pro-active and resourceful emotional states. That's a very valuable skill in the operation of your business.

Also, remember in business, few things are life and death. A short-term financial failure may mean that someone doesn't get paid when they want to; that will rarely kill you or them, especially if you address problems as they happen and don't ignore them. Longer-term financial gaps are also rarely truly catastrophic. Keep in mind that your physical and mental health and, that of your family is really important. Your financial results don't compare with truly life threatening illness or other really catastrophic concerns.

Chapter 13

*Things are Never as Good
as You Think They Are*

Chapter 13

Things are Never as Good as
You Think They Are

I think it was Warren Buffett who explained that the stock market always responds emotionally and that it rarely is accurate. When the market is optimistic, it is overly optimistic, and when it is scared or pessimistic, everything is gloom and doom. Really, the emotional response always overreacts on both ends of the spectrum. That's the source of contrarian investing. When the market is exuberant, then sell. When the market is panicked, buy.

Think of your emotional responses to your day-to-day business activities in the same way. Usually they work the same way as described above. When things are going well, you are on the top of the world and can do no wrong. Probably, when you emotionally are on the top of the world, is really when the unexpected can happen. Be aware, don't take unnecessary risks, and be careful about buying that new house, car, boat, etc.

It's a huge mistake to assume during your best month or year that things will continue to grow at that pace. Don't get me wrong. Continue to plan for growth and success, just don't take it for granted. Your best month of the year may just be your best month ever. Your best year may be a peak not a continuing growth trend.

There's a great ad that I saw for an insurance company. It shows a long tunnel with a light at the end. The caption says: *We never forget that it may be an oncoming train.* Without becoming defeatist that's something good to keep in mind before committing to higher expenses or a more extravagant lifestyle.

Chapter 14

*Landlords and Other People
Who Want to Bleed You Dry*

Chapter 14

Landlords and Other People Who Want to Bleed You Dry

You are the only person who can protect your "bottom line." Lots of suppliers will sell you anything that you are willing to be sold.

The advertising rep will sell you as much advertising with high hopes that you are willing to buy.

Your landlord will let you commit to $5,000, $8,000 or $10,000 per month in rent without batting an eye. And, don't forget about that personal guarantee for the lease payment for three, five or seven years. Really take a very close look at every financial commitment and take care of yourself as the first priority.

You really can't blame the sellers. They are doing their job selling their space, real estate, advertising space, building services, electronic gear, etc.

All of us make bad decisions from time to time and splurge on something we really didn't need, but wanted for whatever reason. Always be careful about increasing your financial commitments. Never expect anyone else to look out for your own interests.

Chapter 15

*Don't Confuse "Activity"
with "Accomplishment"*

Chapter 15

Don't Confuse "Activity"
with "Accomplishment"

Clearly everything else being the same, more activity is better than less, and most martial arts school owners fail to work hard enough on the right activities. A key concern should always be that you focus on the right activities and never confuse "being busy" with effectiveness.

Always ask yourself: Does this contribute to enrollments, renewals, or retention? If the answer is no, then it may just be an activity with little merit.

Now obviously, there are administrative needs for your school. Paying the electric bill and completing forms for the IRS does little to contribute to the items listed above, and clearly must be taken care of regularly. But on an on-going basis, minimize your time on administrative activities and on anything that does not directly contribute to improving your income.

1. Personally handling tasks that should be handled by someone else. Examples are:
   Personal items that should be outsourced
   a. Changing your oil
   b. Doing your own laundry
   Business items that should be outsourced
   a. Handling billing that should be delegated to a billing company.
   b. Doing accounting work that should be delegated to a bookkeeper.
   c. Doing IRS and other reporting for payroll that should be delegated to a payroll service.
   Personally handling items that should be delegated to a staff member:
   a. Running trivial errands like picking up office supplies, etc.
   b. Doing manual labor around the school.

Wasting time during school hours by:
   a. Spending unnecessary time on small talk with a student
   b. Spending time doing administrative work during primetime hours.

2. Participating in lots of "sales" conferences (i.e. Enrollment or Renewal) without closing the sale. Zig Ziglar says that the difference between a professional visitor and a professional sales person is asking for the sale.

3. Expecting prospects who say they'll think it over and get back to you to actually think it over and get back to you. Then, following up consistently.

4. Sitting at your computer when there are students in the school.

5. Calling back ANYONE who is not a student or a prospective student during prime business hours.

6. Running around to local karate tournaments, judging or competing or "supporting your students".

7. Doing personal training during class hours.

8. Answering every telephone call personally.

Quick Read: "Top Performance,"
and "See You at the Top,"
by Zig Ziglar

Chapter 16
Simplify, Simplify, Simplify

Chapter 16

Simplify, Simplify, Simplify

Whenever and wherever possible, figure out ways to simplify your life and your business operation.

You really MUST be diligent, because the natural tendency in any business is to gradually add new procedures and new processes that slowly complicate things without any real conscious effort to do so. Over the years, you accumulate a series of small additions that lead to creeping complexity in your operation.

You must go back to a basic premise of school operations. There are only three important variables: Enrollments, Retention and Tuition. Any time that you, one of your employees, an advisor, your accountant, or your attorney suggests a new procedure or a new filing or recordkeeping system, sit back and think, "does this add to how much I can charge, how long the average student will stay with me, or with how many new students I will enroll?"

In the computer age, your school management software and your accounting software should help you maintain records of just about anything you may ever need to keep. Once paper has been turned into a digital record, get rid of it if at all possible. I know that you are required to keep some records physically for the I.R.S., for your local tax authorities and for a variety of other reasons. But really, you have to keep A LOT less than you may think once you have accurate computer records. Always ask: What's the worst thing that could happen if I just throw this stuff away? Make your own decisions, but sometimes tax records do you more harm than good. I had a sales tax audit recently. My computer records were impeccable and my hard copy backups had long since been disposed of, and we came out clean as a whistle, no problems.

Your attorney, too, may want you to keep all kinds of complicated records. Certainly some of that stuff is really necessary because of the probability of having a problem and the severity of the potential problem. Again, ask him or her what's the worst thing that can happen if I don't keep these records?

Ultimately, paper tends to take on a life of it's own, and grow disproportionate to it's value. Fight this trend in any way possible. Move all your records into your computer systems, and eliminate or discard just about any paper that is possible.

I've gone to a new filing system with my contracts: they get filed chronologically. In other words I have a stack on the shelf by my desk on which the latest contract goes on top. If there ever is any question about a contract I just pull up the information in Master-Vision. If I ever had an issue where I needed the signed original, I can always find it by looking in the section for the month that they were enrolled.

Do you really need to file exam forms, old I.D. cards, report cards or any of the other paper that you organize with great effort?

It may seem trivial, but gradually you start using real valuable time and eventually start hiring people to manage the huge flow of paperwork, most of which has no marginal value to the three biggest issues:

1. How many enrollments you will do
2. How long you will keep your students
3. How much you can charge

At the next level, consider the many little things that add up to unnecessary complications in your business.

One step that I took was to eliminate patches and to have all uniforms screened by the manufacturer before shipping them to me. Again, it may seem trivial ,but inventorying several different patches and reordering takes time and mental energy. Use your time and focus your energy on enrollments, retention and adding value to your students. Don't waste your energy on anything else. How about pads? Can your students buy three styles in two colors each, or do you have a standard required option? Trim, Trim, Trim the number of inventory items that you stock whenever possible without losing sales.

While we are at it, take a look at your personal life. The more you grow, the more likely it is that your personal possessions will start to own you rather than the other way around. Bigger and more does not mean better. Simplify. Really, you may be a lot happier.

Chapter 17

Why Am I Doing This to Myself?

Chapter 17

Why Am I Doing This to Myself?

A couple of years ago I sat back and evaluated my life and business, and ended up asking myself, "Why am I doing this to myself?"

From an outsiders view I had an incredible operation:

1. The Mile High Karate Classic, NASKA "AAA" rated with the top competitors in North America, with international respect, and 1,000 to 1,300 competitors annually. Not to mention a sold-out finals show each year.
2. Five beautiful Sschools, each with 2,500- to 4,800-square-feet in prime locations.
3. 1,200-plus active students.
4. 40-plus paid staff members, including over 30 Black Belts on staff.
5. Black Belt retreats with 350-plus participants.
6. Two huge Black Belt Extravaganzas per year, with 1,500 to 3,500 spectators.
7. Three huge Intramural Tournaments per year, with 500 to 800 competitors.
8. Huge seminars and twice-a-year Black Belt University and Intensive Weekend Training Sessions.
9. A myriad of other events and activities.
10. $1.5 to $2 MILLION gross revenue per year.
11. $120,000 to $180,000 marketing budget annually.
12. Speaking engagements at EFC Seminars and other events throughout the year.

From my perspective:

1. Three staff meetings per week and, countless hours of staff training and supervision.
2. 45-plus weekends per year taken up with local, regional and national tournaments, black belt exams, retreats, seminars, intramurals, speaking engagements or other events.
3. Endless sleepless nights trying to cover $20,000 to $35,000 in payroll TWICE a month.
4. Endless employee problems, such as hiring, training, supervising, disciplining and firing.
5. Huge potential liabilities incurred by a huge staff.
6. Sleepless nights worrying about having a blizzard or some other catastrophe occur on the same day of the National Tournament, with $50,000 to $75,000 in expenses incurred regardless of how many people showed up.
7. 6- or 7-day weeks with 70 to 100 hour work weeks.

What did I change? Just about everything.

1. I "retired" from being a tournament promoter. (I love the NASKA competitors and promoters and I will do anything to support the circuit. But will no longer go to every national event or promote a large event myself.)
2. I rolled back the number of events. Now I do:
   - 1 black belt extravaganza each year, not twol
   - 1 black belt retreat each year, not twol
   - A few extra seminars and other activitiesl
   - 3 intramurals each year.

   I work about five weekends per year, rather than 40.
3. I closed two schools.
4. I restructured the staffing situation to have 13 schools be "owner-operated," Where I get my income "off the top." They pay the bills, pay the staff and keep what's left over.

I now have to directly supervise 13 individuals through one meeting per week. They are "owner-operators" and highly motivated to implement new ideas.

5. I stopped working Saturdays or Sundays with few exceptions.
6. I put my "student" cap back on and began re-exploring direct marketing, copywriting, etc.
7. I renewed several strong industry friendships and solidified my networking follow-up with those individuals.

What was the end result?
1. My workweek was cut in half.
2. I don't work weekends.
3. My income DOUBLED.
4. I suddenly have "hobbies" again.
5. Things are FUN again.

What's the moral? Well for one: "Be careful what you wish for — you may get it"

For another: The only proper judge of the success of your life and lifestyle is you.

I have two former employees and students who have opened their own schools. Their situations are much different.

One made a huge effort to replicate my operation in Denver. Opened multiple locations, developed a huge staff, with high expenses and high grosses, and decided to promote a big tournament.

The other opened one nice school and works 20 to 30 hours per week. Spends lots of time with his kids, coaches their teams, helps at school and spends lots of quality time on non-business related activities.

Which one is more successful?

Well, one has HUGE amounts of stress; huge liabilities; is out of shape, and has mediocre health. Travels a lot for business. Makes a decent income, with lots of ups and downs.

The other makes a similar income without the negatives.

Chapter 18

Hiring from Within

Chapter 18

Hiring from Within

Everyone knows that you should "grow your own" staff and instructors, but often we forget the lessons that are plainly obvious. This is certainly a rule that can be broken from time to time, but let me again remind you what you already know:

1. Martial artists as employees tend to be very "self-righteous:"
   a. Doing anything just to make money "off the students" is bad, and;
   b. They never get paid enough, and;
   c. They don't want anything to do with sales or marketing, only teaching what they want to teach to students they feel like teaching.

2. Unfortunately martial arts is very much like a "cult". Whoever "brainwashed" someone first about what the "True Way" is often owns their heart and soul forever.

3. As a teacher, often you can do no wrong to a dedicated student.

4. As an employer, often you can do nothing right to a mediocre employee.

Take some of these tendencies and exacerbate them with non-homegrown martial artists, and you can easily triple your headaches and cut your results in half.

Remember a few obvious truths:

1. If someone failed once already running their own school, why should working for you be any different? Remember, business owners have LOTS of reasons to be much more self-motivated than anyone's employee.

   If you take a school operator and have a position where they can just teach, if that is something they are really strong at, and not have to market or sell, then it might work. But, failed school operators usually make failed employees. I hate to admit that I've made this mistake a couple of times too many. I'm just a slow learner on some things, I guess.

2. If someone holds allegiance to another instructor or style in their heart, then their true feelings will show in all student and staff interactions. Do you want students excited about the old (read: "real") instructor and their old (read: "true") style, or do you want your students excited about you and your school.

How do you grow your own?

This is a huge subject and better covered in greater detail elsewhere. If you are really interested, rush out and buy the Kovar's *Martial Arts Career Training Manual*.

A few pointers:

1. Look for potential future employees in the introductory classes you teach.

2. Have GREAT retention. If no one gets to Black Belt, there aren't many Black Belts to hire.

3. Have a huge SWAT (assistant instructor) team and special leadership training classes.

4. Take promising candidates "under your wing" personally and guide them to:
   a. increasing leadership;
   b. accelerated progress;
   c. a winning personal appearance;
   d. escalating responsibility;
   e. a vision of a career in the martial arts.

5. Have a goal-oriented career path:
   a. Master Club (or Black Belt Club);
   b. Assistant Instructor;
   c. Instructor;
   d. Head Instructor;
   e. Program Director;
   f. Branch Manager;
   g. School Owner.

6. For teenagers, create a career prospect while paying comparable or slightly better than their other opportunities.

7. For adults:
   a. Consider hiring at early stages of their training for program director or receptionist roles;
   b. Create a career vision that is exciting;
   c. Don't transition volunteers into paid employees unless it is into full time salaried/incentives position;
   d. Do keep the door open for them to open their own school with your help, when and if they want to and are ready.

Chapter 19

*Separate Your EGO
from Your Business*

Chapter 19

Separate Your EGO from Your Business

When you decide to become a school owner, you really must decide to become a businessman and entrepreneur. You no longer are just a martial artist, competitor and teacher. You now must wear lots of hats that may be totally unfamiliar, uncomfortable or just know what you are very good at — at least initially.

One of the biggest failings that martial artists have in general is an EGO that engulfs everything else.

Until you let go of how great you think you are, and start learning from anyone who has something to teach, you will ALWAYS languish in mediocrity.

To separate your ego from your business consider the following:

1. Anytime you are in the company of other school owners or other business owners learn to SHUT UP. Ask questions, listen, find out what they do well and figure out "how they think" about things.

2. When you ask someone for advice, ask a question, listen to the answer, then ask them what questions you should be asking. Avoid, at all costs, telling them everything about yourself. By the time you get done, they just may be out of time or out of patience!

3. Create your school to provide a nice first impression for intros, and a quality learning environment for your students — not to impress other martial artists, other school owners, or your friends and family.

4. Forget what you think you know, and become a real student of every aspect of running your business.

5. Don't be afraid to look dumb or ignorant. Ask questions. Seek new information. Find people who are better at EVERYTHING than you are and be a humble student.

6. Remember that at your school, you are an EDUCATOR, not an ATHELETE or COMPETITOR. Never try to compete with your students. Make your goal that while you maintain your own skills, you teach them to surpass you in any way possible.

7. Don't pretend to know all the answers. Let your Black Belts, staff and students contribute their ideas and expertise. You'll be way ahead.

8. Take the blame for failures yourself, and share the credit for success with everyone.

Chapter 20

The 10 "Secrets" of Leadership

Chapter 20

The 10 "Secrets" of Leadership

There are many effective styles of leadership. Probably, as many different effective styles of leadership as there are different personality types of employees and bosses.

That having been said, I do believe that there are several "secrets" to leadership in any organization:

Vision

You must have a clear and compelling VISION for the future of your organization. I'm not talking about benchmarked goals here, or a target gross or active count, but something much more powerful.

Your vision is a picture of where you want the organization to end up, of the big picture, of how it should look, in as much sensory rich detail as possible.

Leadership starts from within. If you have a clear picture of where you want the organization to end up, then your conversation, actions and goals will tend to fall in line with this vision and ultimately manifest itself.

Communication

Having a clear vision of the future is value-less unless you become exceedingly effective at communicating that vision to others. That does NOT mean that you have to be a gifted public speaker. Many great leaders (including Thomas Jefferson, among others) were not gifted speakers. You may communicate your vision through pictures, public speeches, written communications or ANY media as long as your message gets through to the intended recipients in as compelling a way as possible.

Emotional Commitment

You must lead people from their heart and not their head. Daily commitment comes from an emotional attachment to the leader, to the mission, to the vision or to the target feelings conveyed by your vision of the future. All leadership is based upon the emotional commitment of the followers much more than an abstract intellectual understanding of goals and objectives.

Values Based

Although financial rewards help motivate or help maintain motivation, ultimately people will get out of bed early and work late with the highest levels of intensity for contribution to others and contribution to the community. If financial rewards are directly tied to personal contribution to others, then motivation will remain high. Long-term motivation in any WIN-Lose environment is nearly impossible. Be clear on your overriding values and, operate on a daily basis within those espoused values.

Congruence

Your words and actions must be congruent. You cannot motivate people to contribute and encourage them to a higher purpose if ultimately your integrity is questionable. Although we've seen managers — and, certainly politicians — attain high levels with questionable integrity, I maintain that long-term leadership must be based upon honesty and the highest integrity. If your manager co-opts your help to cover up his extramarital affairs, how much trust will you give him? If your boss has a different persona in public than in private, will you trust their communications with you to be sincere?

Team Orientation

Someone said once: *You can accomplish anything if you don't care who gets credit for it.* In the martial arts, this attitude is exceptionally rare. Many "Master" Instructors have really started to believe their own press, and to act as if anything good that happens to them was their idea. GIVE Credit. Involve the entire team. Work as much as possible to accomplish new directions through consensus. You are better as the leader to play a support role in many discussions and let the team members find the "means" to accomplish the "ends" in your vision.

Results Orientation

Focus on results, NOT process. Create accountability from every team member and student for the end result not the activity. Many ideas are good, if implemented effectively. The greatest idea will fail if implemented poorly. Allow people, within limits, to choose their own means to your agreed-upon end. Manage based upon results, not based upon activity.

Goals

Once all of the other pieces are in place, have daily, weekly, monthly, quarterly and yearly goals. Make sure that they are all congruent with your mission, values and vision. Peter Drucker once said: "What gets measured gets done." Keep records and statistics on everything in your business, but boil your operation down into 2, 3 or 4 key numbers, and then watch them like a hawk. Graph them. Post them in your office, at the reception desk, in the employee break room, or even on the front door of the school. Nothing motivates action like a huge graph of your target active count in plain view. Look at your key numbers daily or even hourly to maintain focus.

Walk Your Talk

I know this is redundant, but really, nothing de-motivates employees or students like hypocrisy. Make a decision to live by your values and to really be who you say you are 24 hours per day, 7 days per week.

Fairness

Ultimately, everyone must benefit from success and must suffer from failure. In compensation, reward people greatly for successes, and make sure they have consequences for failure. If you really delegate authority, focus on the team and allow your staff responsibility, then they must take 100% of the responsibility for their outcomes. Be supportive, but not paternalistic. If you never allow anyone to fail, you've never allowed them to achieve much either.

Quick Read: "Leadership Secrets of the Rogue Warrior," by Richard Marchinko

---

Quick Read: "Leaders," by Warren Bennis and Burt Nanus

Quick Read: "Leadership When the Heat's On," by Danny Cox and John Hoover

---

Quick Read: "The Westpoint Way of Leadership," by Col. Larry Donnithorne

Chapter 21
Open Book Management

Chapter 21

Open Book Management

Although others may disagree with me, I do not believe in secrets.

I mean that in the most complete sense of the word. If you operate with an "open book" policy, then you give employees the tools they need to support your efforts. Withholding data handicaps those same efforts.

Example: A friend owns a rather large school. He has many instructors on his payroll. Although an explicit goal of his staff is to improve student retention, he never shares the most important numbers with them: Active Count, Monthly Enrollment Numbers or Monthly Drop Out Numbers. How can anyone work towards a target that they cannot see?

Many owners that I've seen who feel that they should hid the real numbers from their staff are operating on one of several principles:

1. If they really knew how well I was doing financially, they'd all want more money

Very substantial studies have been conducted on this very subject. The results were conclusive: If employees do not know what each other makes, then they will tend to overestimate what others get paid and underestimate their own total compensation.

If employees do not know what the management makes, they will tend to dramatically overestimate what management gets paid and radically underestimate their own compensation relative to contribution.

Finally, if you are trying to minimize everyone's income but your own may work in the short term, but in the long term, you will have the unintended consequence of this false economy, and everyone who is really valuable will be compensated well — by someone else!

Everyone who is really worth less than you are paying them will stay forever. Therefore, you will eventually degrade the quality of your staff to the point that your results continually fall rather than rise.

2. If they really knew how bad things were, they'd be floating resumes all over town by tomorrow morning.

I have a rather radical world-view on this. Lie to your employees, and they'll not only figure it out, but will lose all respect for you. Tell them the truth, and let the chips fall where they may, then anyone valuable will redouble their efforts to see your organization be successful.

To expand on this even further, SHARE YOUR PAIN. I really don't believe in sharing the wealth in good times, then holding in all of the pain during bad times. Everyone is in the same boat. If the boat is sinking, then pass out bailing buckets, or help everyone into the life rafts. If your staff is held responsible and accountable, then in many cases, probably a lot more than you would suspect, they will rise to the occasion.

3. If my employees know my numbers, eventually my competitors will know my numbers.

In some cases, this may be true, but for most businesses, really, so what? If you are trying to maintain an image that is really false, then it won't last very long, anyway. Certainly, there are times when there really are business secrets that must be protected, but they really are few and far between. And, protecting those secrets may cost you more in lost productivity than their disclosure would cost you. If in doubt, be open and honest with everyone.

4. If my employees know my numbers, eventually the IRS will know my numbers.

If you really are trying to hide significant amounts of money from the IRS or anyone else, then I guess you should keep in mind that you are at risk if ANYONE but yourself knows or could accurately guess what's going on. You'll have to make your own decisions here, however, my policy since day one has been HONESTY. I don't mind telling you that ANYTHING I can possibly justify writing off will get written off. And, given a choice of a trip to a nice place with any business purpose and one purely for pleasure — well, who doesn't want to write off everything that is legal.

As for HIDING and EVADING, well, there is always a risk of your wife becoming your ex-wife in a nasty divorce. Of your senior person deciding that you don't share the wealth enough and looking for a way to stab you in the back. Really, for me, lying just takes too much effort. Be truthful and skip having to worry about this stuff.

5. I am the one with all the answers. I study the numbers, then tell them what to do and actively manage their activities.

I don't expect my employees to turn off their brains at the door. Hopefully, everyone has A LOT of good ideas. They may need to be directed and tempered by my experience or big-picture view. But, if your staff is not contributing, you might as well have computers and robots run your business.

After all of the above, I believe in something sincerely: As long as I am fair in proportionate compensation and honest in my interactions, then the more information I share honestly, the more everyone around me will have an opportunity to contribute to my operation.

Never discount where the next blockbuster idea may come from. With adequate information people who you never thought could contribute, will and in a BIG way.

Quick Read: "Open Book Management," by John Case

Quick Read: "The Great Game of Business," by Jack Stack

Chapter 22

*The Real Secrets of Wealth
in a Martial Arts School*

Chapter 22

The Real Secrets of Wealth in a Martial Arts School

The real secret of wealth in a martial arts school is student retention and loyalty.

If your students absolutely LOVE what you do, then they are prone to:

1. Pay more for classes.
2. Stay as a paying student for a much longer period of time.
3. Add the entire family.
4. Bring all of their friends.
5. Become a loyal and enthusiastic volunteer for your school.
6. Become an assistant instructor.
7. Be a staff prospect.

Schools that have EXCELLENT retention rates make EXPONTIALLY more money to the bottom line than do schools that have to constantly struggle to keep their students happy. If you were to apply yourself 100% to one area that would make a huge difference for your school, that should be: get GREAT at keeping your students in class and excited, forever!

- Become an excellent educator.
- Become a legendary motivator.
- Develop impeccable, human relations skills.
- Get to know everyone by name, including mom, dad, sister, grandmother, etc.
- Have tremendous student progress.
- Be liked and likable.
- Be honest and sincere.

CARE DEEPLY and PERSONALLY about your students every day.

Quick Read: "The Loyalty Effect," by Reichheld

Chapter 23
Learn from the Real *Experts*

Chapter 23

Learn fmor the **Real** *Experts*

"Just ignore the man behind the curtain..."
— The Great and Powerful Oz

In your quest for knowledge, there are two contradictory principles, both of which are important to recognize and follow:

First, there are many people who tout themselves as experts in every industry who really don't know all that much about the day-to-day intricacies of running your type of business. They've either never really been there on the firing line doing the job on a daily basis the way that you are, or at one time they ran a very mediocre business. Possibly after having never had much success themselves, they decide to teach others how to be a huge success.

Second, in most sports, it is rare for a good player to make a good coach and vise versa. Business and teaching consulting follows some similar trends. In other words, some of the guys who are really good at what they do daily may not have the ability to explain their success in any sort of effective way. Additionally, they may not have the ability to coach you on to success. Remember if they are really making a huge income running their business, it may not be worth their time to try to teach you how to do the same thing — certainly not without lots of leverage. That is through a book or video as opposed to one-on-one.

Now, as I've said, these really are contradictory principles. However, in your quest for knowledge, I think it is very important to at least understand who and what you are dealing with, and evaluate all information received from that context.

If you are dealing with someone whose only skill is to market their services to others like you, do they really know how to help you achieve more? If you are dealing with someone who is creative at coming up with new ideas in a vacuum and never applying them in the real world, do you really want to invest a lot of effort and time in their untested idea, first?

If you are dealing with someone who looks to be a good coach, how many champions have they produced? If the answer is lots, then look, listen and learn. If the answer is none, look somewhere else. You may be working with someone ready to bloom, but why waste your time and effort on an unproven quantity?

If you are dealing with someone who's claim to fame is their huge success in running their own operation, try to "look behind the curtain" to see if their success was real or illusory. Did they have the type of operation that you want to imitate, or was their operation more for show than for substance?

What's the best approach?

1. Find people who are running a really good operation and MODEL their successes. Keep in mind that just because someone is good at marketing doesn't mean they are good at teaching, retention or service. Model small segments of successful operations and make sure you don't model the things that they are screwing up.

Keep in mind that modeling is looking, watching and measuring what REALLY gets done, and not what the owner tells you he or she is doing. Then, benchmark that behavior and copy it as closely as possible. It is possible that they really don't know what they are doing successfully and maybe you can help them understand it better with your study. I've worked with some very excellent schools where I ultimately had to explain to them what it was they were doing to get the results that they were getting.

2. Find coaches with a proven track record. Listen to their advice. Be diligent in your application.

3. Be a student, have lots of sources of information and apply what seems to work for you. In the martial arts industry there are LOTS of sources of information. Everyone distributes some great stuff and, everyone distributes some watered down mediocre ideas. Always work to have access to as many sources of information as possible. Keep what works for you and discard everything else.

4. Always get REAL numbers. Use them to evaluate the efficacy of any idea or concept.

A couple of things to watch out for:

1. When a coach tries to explain what someone else is doing successfully, it is always better to go to the source and figure out reality.Often the advice or description that you get is filtered and inaccurate. That inaccuracy has several sources.

   a. Every human summarizes, filters and redefines communications based upon their own perspective and prejudices. What they heard may not really be what's happening. Or, by the time they communicate the idea to you it may have permutated beyond recognition.

   b. Everyone has their own agenda. Their objective in communicating with you may have more to do with selling you on what ever their current agenda is than in relaying to you accurate information.

   c. Watch for "fluff" and "hype"; often, reality is not nearly so glorious as it would seem. There are often additional factors that are not readily apparent or quickly communicated.

2. Avoid untested ideas. Ideas are easy. Any of us can have hundreds of seemingly brilliant ideas every week.

Over the years, I've spent lots of money and tons of hours implementing my ideas. Of course, I was convinced that each one was brilliant.

Ultimately, it's your market and your customers who will tell you if your idea is a hit or a blooper. Test everything. If it works, keep doing it, and then tell lots of people. If it falls on it's face, have a nice quick failure and a wonderful learning opportunity. Then bury it deep. Learn and move on.

If someone else is sharing or selling you on their brilliant idea, always ask the question:

Has this been implemented successfully? If so, by whom?

Then, call the reference and find out what really happened. If things pan out, then by all means implement it aggressively. But, make sure you don't implement half, three quarters or even ninety% of an idea. Get all of it. Do it A-Z.

I've seen lots of ads and other ideas touted as "tested." Always ask: by whom? What happened? Let me see the numbers.

Example: Your billing or consulting company sends you their latest "tested" ad. You ask them how it worked, and they say so-and-so used this ad and got 20 calls last week! Nice information, but you are still rather clueless aren't you? Well, did they spend $10,000 running the ad in every major venue, and it pulled at $500 per call. Or, did they spend $500 in the penny saver and ended up at $25 per call. That extra bit of information makes a difference, doesn't it. Also, did they get 20 calls and 15 enrollments, or did they get 20 calls and no enrollments? How qualified were these prospects? And need I mention, is the number really 20, or is that exaggerated by a factor of 2, 5 or 10?

3. Keep the political context in mind. Always evaluate any idea or communication based upon who's trying to look good and what's in it for them.

4. Take PUBLIC statements with a grain of salt. I've had the misfortune to stand in a seminar as a key speaker, "behind the curtain," talking with other speakers about what they really do and don't do in their operation on a daily basis. Then I listened to them on the podium contradict themselves aggressively, or, in my world-view, lie

to the audience about what is making them successful to avoid rocking the boat or contradicting a prevailing political agenda.

In almost any seminar, convention, or other presentation there is an underlying political agenda going on. In 99.999% of the cases, the underlying bias is never explicitly outlined for the attendees.

Ask yourself who is promoting this convention or seminar. What are their best interests? If the seminar is promoted by a billing company, their objective will be for as close to 100% of your revenue as possible to flow through their company. They may have little incentive for your net to be strong, but huge incentive for your gross to continue to grow through any means possible. If the seminar is promoted by an equipment supplier, they will likely have lots of incentive for you to focus on retail, pro shops and training aids. If the seminar is promoted by a "consulting group," they are highly motivated to prove how smart they are, to present lots of new (and often untested ideas) and to continue to re-sell you on the value of their advice and support.

Chapter 24

Always Follow the Money

Chapter 24

Always Follow the Money

Just to expand from last chapter, prior to accepting any idea, concept or procedure, ask who's trying to sell me this idea, and what's in it for them? This idea applies in many settings both micro and macro.

Outside our industry, for every medical discovery and every great news article, ask yourself who really stands to benefit the most from this research, discovery or new drug. Did they fund the study? Are they a big advertiser with this particular news outlet?

In almost every institution, whether it be government or private funded, ultimately there is a political and a financial agenda. For every new opinion, statistic and discovery, look underneath to see who is pushing the concept, and where the funding came from, before buying into that news story, statistical report or medical breakthrough.

Within our industry keep in mind who's making the suggestion and what's in it for them:

An advertising agency: They usually get paid a%age of your advertising budget. Therefore, to them, some advertising is good, more is better, a huge amount is fantastic. When it comes to results they will remind you of the IMAGE you are building, the BRANDING that you are accomplishing, and the RECALL of your ads. All of that jargon can be translated as follows:

"We didn't help you sell anything, but you should keep spending money because one day you might," or, more accurately, "We want to suck as much money out of your wallet as possible, as quickly as possible, for as long as possible, and everything else is secondary."

The above applies as well to everyone who wants to sell you advertising including newspaper advertising, Yellow pages, radio, television, Valpak, etc.

Remember, to them, you tracking your results is a negative. It means that they have to perform and that you will hold them accountable.

A billing company: "It's illegal to accept cash up front for your lessons."

"90% (60%, 70%, 80%) of your revenue should be monthly billing." Translation: "We want to make a%age on as much of your revenue as possible."

"EFT won't work." Translation: "We don't want you to do that because you can cut us out of the loop too easily."

Consulting or Billing Company: "This new ad is fantastic. It's tested. You can't go wrong. It was developed by an expert!" Translation: "We hope that you are impressed so that you'll want us to keep sending you stuff like it;" or, "That college kid is an expert on his Mac and he thinks the ad looks really nice. It will be tested — by you! Let us know!"

Now, don't take all this and get too skeptical. There probably are LOTS of people who know more about their area of expertise than you do. Listen to their ideas and, make them count. However, always filter their ideas by their predisposition.

Follow the money.

Chapter 25

Getting Rich Off the Blood
of Your Employees

Chapter 25

Getting Rich OFF the Blood of Your Employees

A common syndrome is for employees to feel that you are getting rich while they slave, sweat and do the real work of the organization. The reality is that employees don't understand two crucial elements in our capitalistic society:

1. With risk comes higher reward and, potential for MUCH greater loss.
2. People tend to earn what they are worth.

So what do you do?

One option is to hide your wealth, pretend that your really don't make much money and that you work much harder than they think you do.

I'm not much for lying and pretending. Reality pretty much always comes out and then you really look hypocritical.

A second option is: Be honest, don't hide your car, watch, house or trips. Do build a career path for your staff. Do share the wealth and, show them how their contribution can enhance their outcomes.

Chapter 26

Aligning Your Interests

Chapter 26

Aligning Your Interests

I heard a cute comment that a business owner made to a prospective employee a few years back:

"Son, I'll help make you rich — *if* you help make me richer"

That pretty much sums up aligning your interests.

Run your business daily with enlightened self-interest. Figure out ways to make each area of concern that you have in your business also be an area of concern for your key staff.

If the school does real well, they should do real well. If it does poorly, they should have some sleepless nights as well.

As an owner what are you concerned about ultimately?

1. Student retention
2. New enrollments
3. Active count
4. Gross revenue
5. Net profit

Always set goals for your staff and create bonuses and pay scales so that your staff's outcomes and your own are very closely aligned.

Many owners foolishly try to keep everyone's income as low as possible, while having an ever widening gulf between their own income and that of their staff.

If someone contributes A LOT and the school has SUCCESS, then SHARE the wealth.

If someone doesn't contribute a lot or if the school is failing, SHARE your pain!

When you are really all focused on the same OUTCOMES rather than the minutia of the processes, then your results and staff harmony will dramatically improve.

Chapter 27

*The "Dramatic Metamorphosis":
Employee vs. Owner*

Chapter 27

The "Dramatic Metamorphosis"
Employee vs. Owner

Something really strange happens when someone goes from being an employee to an owner:

1. As an employee, they complain about 40 hours per week. As an owner they work 75 + without mentioning a thing.
2. As an employee, they must be convinced of "what's in it for them" for every new idea. As an owner, if it will help pay the bills, it's a great idea and they will implement with enthusiasm.
3. As an employee, they must be talked into reading material to help their performance. As an owner, they develop a "thirst for knowledge."

When someone is an owner, they have several positive and negative incentives that an employee does not have:

1. Their name is on the lease (for $200,000 or more), and is expected to be paid, regardless of the results.
2. They are the last one to get paid.
3. They are ultimately responsible for their outcomes.
4. It is difficult to just walk out one day and get a different job.
5. They have "pride of ownership."
6. They will get the credit for their results.
7. They are ultimately in control of their income and have 100% benefit for improved results.

Over and over again, I've seen employees leave to become school owners, or stay and move from salaried employee to school owner. In nearly every case, they immediately doubled their effectiveness.

Often, and it really has been entertaining, as failed employees "proved" that they could really perform on their own. (If they were so good why did they fail for a year on my payroll? Because they could!.)

Any time you can create a feeling of ownership, real or otherwise, in a staff member, their performance will go up. Anytime you can turn a branch manager into an owner, their effectiveness will improve and their longevity will dramatically improve.

Chapter 28

You Can't Teach a Pig to Sing

Chapter 28

You Can't Teach a Pig to Sing

There's an old saying that I first heard it from master trainer and author Danny Cox: "You can't teach a pig to sing. It wastes your time and irritates the pig."

When evaluating employees, keep in mind that there are really only three important factors:

1. **Aptitude**
2. **Skills**
3. **Motivation**

Everything else is superfluous to these three elements.

The first factor is aptitude. This is where your pre-employment screening is important. Some people are great teachers, yet lousy salesmen or marketers. Others may be great in the back room with the books, but for heaven's sake, don't make them talk to real people.

Define the aptitudes necessary for the job function and screen accordingly. If after some period of time, you decide that the person just won't be able to "get it," then the thing you can do that is best for them is to decide quickly and help them transition to a more effective career.

The second factor is skills. This is your most important area of focus. You must train every new staff member on each area that they will be responsible for controlling. And, I'm not talking a broad description and a two-page job description.

Train on every detail in nauseating depth.

Role play. Video tape and audio tape performance. Keep records. Give feedback. Tune and tweak performance. Then, 90 days later, start over. Continue this cycle forever.

Some managers hate to spend this much time or a lot of money, because they are afraid that people will leave, and that effort and money will go to waste. I heard it expressed this way once: "What's worse? A trained employee who leaves, or an untrained one who stays?"

The final factor is motivation. It is certainly possible for someone to have the aptitude and the skills and to not have the interest. Without self-motivation, any employee is pretty much worthless.

Now here's a radical concept as well:

- Everyone brings their own level of motivation to the job.
- Just about everyone is highly motivated to do well when they start.
- Your best result is to do anything you can to stay out of their way and not screw that up!

Now clearly there are ways to enhance this personal motivation. Recognition is great. Money doesn't hurt. Incentives based upon performance is a prerequisite but in general, I really believe that people arrive with motivation, then often we screw that up with silly rules, an unpleasant environment, unfair behavior or through just minimizing the employee's contribution overall.

Chapter 29

Never Stop Learning

Chapter 29

Never Stop Learning

No matter how much you know, there's a lot more to be learned.

- Are you an AGGRESSIVE student?
- How many books have you read this year? (non-fiction)
- Do you take notes when you read?
- Do you write in the books, jot ideas and implementation strategies?
- Do you ever re-read a book 2, 3, 5 or 10 times?
- Do you just LOVE Amazon.com or your local Barnes and Noble or Borders?
- How many biographies have you read?
- How many audio tapes have you purchased and listened to?
- Are you on the Nightingale-Conant preferred customers list?
- Do you get ANY industry specific information you can get?
- Do you subscribe to all of our industry's school materials?
- How many video tapes have your purchased and watched?
- Do you have the Kovar series?
- How many curriculum-oriented tapes do you have?
- How about materials from Zig Ziglar, Jay Abraham, Tony Robbins or Denis Waitly?
- Do you go to many seminars?
- Do you go to every industry-specific seminar you can find?
- How much would you spend for a seminar? Would $2,000, $3,000, $5,000 or $10,000 be too much? Why?
- What types of seminars would you and have you attended. Is it time to "get out of your box" and explore other subjects?
- Have you thought about going back to college?
- Would a BA, BS, MA, MS or MBA be helpful?
- Do you have any MENTORS?
- How often do you talk to that individual?
- Do you know what they are good at and weak at?
- How's your peer networking?
- Do you talk with at least three people per week who are doing something better than you are?
- Do you share ideas and gain them regularly?
- Do you talk to successful people outside your "normal" circle of acquaintances?

The most successful people I know do several things religiously:

1. Read biographies of successful people.
2. Read a lot.
3. Keep a dictionary on their desk and look up words that they are not sure of consistently.
4. Break out of their "paradigm" to look at things in new ways.
5. Talk to people who are more successful than they are.
6. Listen more than they talk.

As soon as you stop being a student you stop growing. Look for new information AND apply it to your business and life. Avoid learning just for it's own sake, but apply that information quickly.

Chapter 30

"Opinions are Like...
Everyone's Got One"

Chapter 30

"Opinions are Like...Everyone's Got One"

Many great ideas were killed by asking someone else's opinion.

Ideas are proven or disproven by aggressive implementation. Any time that you have a "brilliant" idea that doesn't cost much and won't require hundreds of hours — JUST DO IT! If it works, great. Tell your mentors, consultants, peers and friends. If it fails, well, either tune it or, at the very least, don't tell anyone!

More great success was killed by second-guessing every idea, running through the gauntlet of other people's opinions and attempting to be perfect.

As Patton said (or, at least is purported to have said) "I'd rather have a good plan violently executed today, than a perfect one implemented next week."

As a manager, get really good at enhancing and bringing clarity to the ideas of your employees without squashing the initiative and enthusiasm that they bring to it. I've gotten really good recently at this response:

"Gee I don't know if that will work or not, but, if you really think it will, why don't you try it and let us know what happened!"

Often accompanied by:

"A couple of other things that might help would be _____, _____, _____ and _____." My friend _____ _____ has had some real success with something like that. Let's get him/her on the phone and brainstorm the idea a little."

Remember, no matter how good you get at advertising, you will only know if it is a good ad once the phones start to ring (after spending money to place it!).

No matter how great an educator you are, the results that your students have is the only indicator of the quality of your methods.

Results prove whether an idea was a good one or a bad one. No amount of armchair quarterbacking will make any difference.

Reframe Your Worldview

Often, we listen to REALLY good ideas and are unable to HEAR them because they are in conflict with our predispositions.

If you hear an idea that doesn't seem to make sense, try stepping into that person's "frame of reference" for a few minutes and figure out why it makes sense to them. You may find a real gem, and may create some flexibility in your own thinking as well.

A few more reading suggestions:

A Millionaires' Notebook, by Steven Scott; *Built to Last,"* by James Collins and Jerry Porras; *Reframing Organizations,* by Bolman and Deal; *Influence: Science and Practice,* by Robert Cialdini; *Executive EQ,* by Robert Cooper and Ayman Sawaf; *The Loyalty Effect,* by Frederick Reichheld; and, *How to Close Every Sale,* by Joe Girard.

And, anything by Denis Waitley, Zig Ziglar, Tony Robbins, Jay Abraham, Dan Kennedy, Joseph Sugarman or Tom Peters.

Chapter 31

The Quickest Way
to Kill a School

Chapter 31

The Quickest Way to Kill a School

My past columns have often focused on marketing and sales as they relate to your martial arts school. Frankly, this one will also, but, from a 180-degree angle.

What's the quickest way to kill a school? Get really good at sales and marketing without mastering service and education.

Let me say that again, in a different way. If you are not an excellent teacher and motivator, then the absolute worst thing that you can do is expose your school to a huge number of prospective students and let your entire area learn about how bad your school really is in the critical service delivery.

Let me give you this example from a couple of other industry perspectives:

One of the many "marketing gurus" that I've studied is Dan Kennedy (see www.kennedymagnetic.com.). He shares a story about opening a new restaurant. After exploring all of the many advertising options — you know, Val Pak, Money Mailer, Flyers, Direct Mail, etc. — they decide to instead print up certificates good for a free meal (Absolutely free — not 2 for 1, no cost for drinks, etc.). They deliver these certificates to every home and office in their immediate vicinity by hand with a personal invitation to try the restaurant.

What happened is, they were swamped with traffic during their first month, with very little revenue, because they were giving away the lion's share of the meals. What do you expect would happen next?

Well, if this is all I knew, then I would say probably one of two things would happen:

First possibility: There is no business to speak of the second month, or thereafter, and they quickly go out of business.

Second possibility: The second month they are just as busy with happily paying customers and their business quickly grows from there. What's the difference? By now it should be obvious: Good food and fast, friendly service.

If they had good food and fast-friendly service, then their expensive marketing effort was well worth it. If not, they just proved to everyone in their neighborhood that they were bad at what they do, and not worth revisiting for free or otherwise.

How about another example: One of my executive staff members, Dave MacDonald, worked with Grease Monkey for many years. For Grease Monkey, the absolute best strategy to grow a new location was the same one discussed above.

They would distribute certificates widely that were good for a free oil change, with no strings attached.

Once many of their neighbors visited the location and were treated professionally and courteously with quality service, then they are very likely to return again and again for service. This time, paying the standard rate. Again, this strategy would backfire quickly for a poorly run location.

What if the location was poorly maintained, with grumpy staff that performed the service poorly and looked up the customer's skirt while changing the oil?

Well, the word would spread quickly, but not positively. They would be ensured a tough launch, and have difficulty overcoming their reputation.

Our industry has experience this situation often enough that many excellent martial artists who are also excellent teachers and mentors to their students are afraid of developing their own marketing talent or sales skills for fear of becoming like those other "shady operators."

In contrast, I would say that the two biggest sins in our industry are:

First: Quality teachers who are afraid of or unwilling to learn to promote their school and grow their student base.

Second: Lousy martial artists and teachers who master the art of marketing and sales, and therefore, poison the experience of martial arts for their students.

No business ever thrived without mastering three key functions: Marketing, Sales and Service Delivery. Miss any one of these key areas and you are doomed to financial failure.

I highly recommend that you start with a top to bottom overview of your school. Forget for the moment of your own mastery of your chosen art. It's really not very relevant to your student's experience. Focus instead on every aspect of your service delivery, starting with the most important, and then reviewing all of the supporting areas. Start with your rapport with students and their parents, then look at your communications skills. Next, evaluate your ability to properly chunk your curriculum for student mastery. Next, how's the classroom pacing and structure? How about your facilities, training, support equipment and curriculum support materials? How's your appearance and the appearance of your key staff?

After you've reviewed all of these areas, now it's time to really master the marketing and sales functions then grow your student base dramatically.

Chapter 32

"Be Careful What You Wish for...
You May Get It," Part 1

Chapter 32

"Be Careful What You Wish for... You May Get It," Part 1

I've just been sitting down to listen to the audio tapes from my recent boot-camp: "The Summit of Martial Arts Millionaires." During the event I was happy with the quality of people and information being shared, but, frankly, as the host and primary speaker, I didn't really have as much time to listen to and really absorb what my guests were sharing.

Honestly, as I sit here with my nerdy Walkman listening to over 22 hours of content, I am "blown away" by the incredible content.

One of the sessions that I would like to share with you right now was a multi-school owner's session that included Jeff Smith (running three schools in Virginia and formerly General Manager for nine Jhoon Rhee Schools), Bill Clark (running 15 schools in Jacksonville, Florida), Sergio Von Schmeling (running 15 schools in Orlando, Florida), Joe Corley (running multiple schools in Atlanta for over 30 years at six locations), Tim Kovar (running five schools in Sacramento), and, many others, including myself (running five-plus schools in Denver since 1983, currently nine locations).

As I facilitated and lead this two-hour discussion of how to most effectively run multiple locations, one theme surfaced early in the conversation: Most school owners who want to do multiple schools — shouldn't!

You may find it interesting that a conversation among some of the most successful multi-school operators in the country would yield that as one of the first points of consensus. However, let me explain.

Before you even consider opening a second location, ask yourself some penetrating questions:

First, why do I want another location?

Is your motivation to make more money and have more students, or is it to provide a career path for some very competent staff that are being stifled in the current situation? The only real justification that is appropriate is that you are busting at the seams with quality staff and want to provide a career path for them.

If you want to make more money or have more students, you very probably can do that quicker and easier by growing your existing school. I know of single school locations with over 1,000 active students, and I know of at least one school that NETS $500,000 per year. If you haven't exceeded those numbers, you probably haven't maxed out your current location.

Second, am I capable of MANAGING multiple locations?

Step back and really look at your current school operation. Is it systems-driven or purely personality-driven? What happens when you take a week off — do you ever? When you are gone do things just keep clicking along, or does your operation grind to a halt until you get back and make things happen?

If your current location is not systems-driven, two locations will be a disaster. Really document, organize and systematize your existing school. Train your staff. Teach them to follow processes that have been proven while striving for the monthly goals of your school.

Third, is my existing staff focused on our growth objectives, or am I the only one worried about our numbers?

If you have a strong team implementing well-developed systems, striving to hit the growth objectives that you've set for the school, that's great. If not, you'd better get to work on sharing the numbers for the school and creating a team that is focused on your goals, rather than carrying all of the weight yourself. Many school owners that I know are paranoid about sharing any number with their staff.

If your staff members don't know active count, dropout rate, enrollments, renewals, gross and other significant numbers, how can they effectively contribute? I would never have an instructor who wasn't focused on the active count, and who didn't know how many people dropped out, who they were, how many enrollments we added, and how many students upgraded or renewed in a given period of time. I would also never have a program director who was not intimately aware of our intro flow, conversion ratios to enrollment, gross revenue and renewal rates.

Fourth, am I capable of managing a large staff?

Many school owners are excellent motivators and sales people with their students but, aren't good at teaching employees to have those same traits. Once you go from a single-school operator to a multiple-school operator, you forever give up the role of "doer" of the significant school activities and move to the role of "trainer and supervisor" of the significant activities within the school.

It's very important that you evaluate your interests, temperament and perspective to determine if people management and staff development is a strength that you have developed.

Chapter 33

"Be Careful What You Wish for... You May Get It," Part 2

Chapter 33

"Be Careful What You Wish for...You May Get It," Part 2

In the last column I began explaining that most school owners who want to do multiple schools probably shouldn't and gave you a few questions to ask yourself prior to considering a second location.

Those questions were:

1. Why do I want a second location?
2. Am I capable of managing multiple locations?
3. Is my existing staff focused on our growth objectives, or am I the only one worried about our numbers?
4. Am I capable of managing a large staff?

In discussing with my recent panel of Martial Arts Millionaires what the usual outcome is when a school owner opens a second location, I gave my opinion and got unanimous agreement.

That opinion was this: What usually happens is you get a school operator who is doing fairly well (probably because of his/her personality as an instructor) who decides that he will make more money running two schools, and then opens a second location. In 95% of the cases what happens looks something like this:

First location was grossing $20,000, netting $10,000. Second location opens. First location drops from $20,000 per month to $15,000. At the same time that location's expenses increase from $10,000 to $15,000. The second location loses money for quite awhile, then grows to do $15,000, with expenses of $15,000. Now instead of taking home $10,000 per month, the net profit, combined, is $0. Staff is up by three full-time people. Profits are gone. The owner works twice as hard for no money.

Gee, isn't that an exciting picture?

I'm really not trying to be "doom and gloom." I'm just sharing with you that there is more to running multiple schools that being good at the activity of running a school. As a multiple school operator, you really must be a systems designer, people developer and staff supervisor. Okay, so I haven't scared you away from the concept. Maybe you've watched me, Ernie Reyes, Bill Clark, Jeff Smith, Tiger Schulman, or some other chain operator, and really want to move in that direction. How do you get started?

First, make sure your first school is very profitable.

Second, really learn the WHY's of how things work effectively in your school. What makes an exciting class. What's the exact structure of your enrollment process; how can you systematize your marketing; etc.

Third, go to work becoming systems driven. Make sure your first school can continue to run profitably with you gone for a weekn or even a month.

Fourth, learn to be a teacher and coach of staff, not just your martial arts students. Go to work developing your people to be effective marketers, sales people and teachers. Coach them on how to interact with different types of students and parents. Teach them how to work through service recovery and out of the ordinary situations.

Fifth, become extremely goal-focused in your school with all staff. Set daily, weekly and monthly objectives for improving your school in every aspect. Really start "holding their feet to the fire" on achieving your weekly and monthly objectives.

Sixth, create enlightened self-interest in your staff by establishing effective commission structures based upon results. Make sure that all key full-time staff members have a solid financial incentive, and a real career opportunity to share in the success of your school.

Seventh, create a "no-excuses" environment for your staff. Make sure they are accountable and responsible at all times in their areas of responsibility. If you have people who are frequently allowed to miss work, make excuses for failure to accomplish objectives, or who are not truly held accountable, then your problems will multiply when you are "off-site."

If you've done all of these things you will probably begin to see a dramatic improvement in results for your schools. Now if you still intend to open a second school, it's time to start looking for locations.

Where should your second school be located?

There are many factors in this determination, but one that few people think about is this:

It should be as close as possible without taking away market from the first school, and in a location where much of your marketing efforts can benefit both locations. Do not go across town or across the state for your second school. Look to the next significant neighborhood and find a way to locate a second school that is geographically close, but still pulls from a different neighborhood.

Chapter 34

Important Issues for Large Operators

Chapter 34

Important Issues for Large Operators

As your school expands, and you can no longer personally touch and control every aspect of your school operation, there are several important issues that begin to arise that you may never have previously considered. The first of these that I'd like to address is how to insure control as you develop strong Black Belts and strong staff.

Once you expand to multiple locations, or as you grow your single school to a large student body of 300 or more students, you will find it necessary to delegate much, or perhaps all, of the teaching to an employee. In a martial arts school, personal loyalty and respect for the instructor is an important component of our development process. Martial arts schools, especially more traditional schools, depend on a strong hierarchy and on obedience to the instructor.

The same structure that helped you maintain order in the early stages of your growth can become a problem down the line if not managed properly. Industry horror stories abound.

A common story goes like this. First you develop a student, teaching them from white belt through their coveted Black Belt. Next, you begin to teach them leadership skills, and begin allowing them to teach more and more students, and larger and larger chunks of your student body. Often this is in parallel with developing the individual's athletic prowess, and they become a cornerstone of your school and a respected champion of the tournament circuit.

Your confidence having grown in this person's skills and leadership abilities, you offer them a "career" position with you, and they begin teaching for you full-time. Gradually they become the head instructor, and teach most of the classes, while you become increasing focused on the sales, marketing and administrative aspects of your school. Gradually, your students begin seeing your Black Belt as their primary teacher and mentor, and the teacher starts to take great pride in "his" student's achievement.

What comes next is often that this instructor begins to hear from students that he should have his own school. Perhaps he gets married and his wife continually complains that he should have his own school, and that he's not getting paid enough, and, of course, that he is responsible for the success of the school, since all the owner does is sit in the office and talk to people all day.

Then one day, like a lighting bolt out of the blue…

Well, you can probably finish the story. I've seen cases where your previously loyal Black Belt employee has moved across the street, and in one case, actually announced at the monthly belt test that the students should join him across the street on Monday. Perhaps followed by letters and phone calls to solidify the solicitation of your clientele.

The question becomes, how do you protect yourself against such a disaster?

Well, there are many ways that school operators attempt to protect themselves. The ways that don't work are for you to always be the students' primary contact ,and to aggressively work to make sure you are always seen as the top athlete, teacher and main student contact. That approach is fine up to 100 or 150 students, but, then you've got to delegate and let others take some responsibility.

What must happen, then, are several things.

First, your school must be built on a formal hierarchy, with you visible at the top. It must always be clear that you are the senior person in your school and that all others report to you. This area is where larger organizations and affiliations often help to solidify everyone's relative position.

Second, before hiring anyone, it is important to have a clear understanding. That written understanding must include several things.

A. You are enthusiastic about helping this budding martial arts instructor grow into a substantial career in the martial arts.

B. Your willingness to help him grow in anyway possible.

C. Your willingness to continually compensate his relative to his contribution to the financial outcomes in your school.

D. His commitment to now and always gives the support to you and your school.

E. HIs understanding that it is unacceptable to ever teach any of YOUR students outside of your school environment and that regardless of how the future unfolds he will never solicit any of your students.

F. His understanding that it is acceptable for him to open their own school in the future under your banner or independently, but that he will never open within a reasonable distance, so as not to compete with you, or you to compete with him.

In conclusion, there are many landmines to avoid as your school grows. Developing your own competition is certainly one that is important to control and monitor.

Chapter 35

*How Much Can You Spend
to Generate an Enrollment?*

Chapter 35

How Much Can You Spend to Generate an Enrollment?

Everyone has heard that you should spend approximately 10% of your gross revenue on advertising. However, that doesn't answer many important questions about how to *structure* your marketing for your school. Even within the 10% number, some of the very TOP schools in the country vary from zero% direct advertising budget up to as much as 20%. How do you figure out what to do specifically?

Ultimately, you must start with a number of what you are able to pay for an ENROLLMENT, then track your enrollment ratios and figure out, if for some reason it's important to you, what you can pay for a call. And, how much you have to spend monthly to hit your target numbers?

How much you can afford to spend for an enrollment ultimately boils down to two factors:

Student Retention Rate and Your Tuition Rate.

This may not be what you expected, however, how much you will be willing to pay for an enrollment will be greatly dependent upon what the average enrollment is worth to you over the lifetime of their participation in your school.

Let me give you two extreme, but real, examples:

First. A school operates a kickboxing program that has an average student life span of three months. In other words, 33% drop out per month. To maintain approximately 200 active students, they must enroll 600 new members per year. Their average monthly tuition per student is $49, for an average lifetime value per new member of $147.

Second. A school operates a very solid martial arts program that has an average student lifespan of 33 months. Three% of their students drop

out on a monthly basis. Their monthly tuition averages $130 per month. Their average lifetime value per new member exceeds $4,000.

In the first example, what would you be willing to pay for a new student? Well if you kept your student acquisition cost to 10%, then you would be able to spend $14.70 per enrollment.

In the second example, at 10%, you would be willing to pay over $400 per new enrollment.

If, from a particular media source, your conversion ratio from call to enrollment is 50%, then you would be able to pay $200 per call.

See from these examples what a huge difference tuition rate and student longevity make on your thinking?

When the Tae Bo and cardio kickboxing craze came along, I have to admit that it began to peak my interest. Why? Cheap info calls. I threw a couple of ads out and started getting $5, $10 and $15 info calls. That looked really great. However, after a few months, I realized the huge gap in the economics between my traditional martial arts program and this cardio craze.

Now I know that quite a few schools had some success with this, but what I saw most often was successful martial artists taking their eye of the ball on their traditional program, lured by the sexiness and popularity of the cardio craze. I saw some schools with strong volumes of 400, 500 or 600 cardio students really only making $5,000 to $10,000 gross per month from the cardio program. If you can do that without disrupting your regular program, then fine. However, this was often a matter of giving up dollars to chase dimes (or even pennies).

Let's take the above discussion to a couple of more layers of complexity.

First, if we are to keep our average marketing budget to around 10% of our gross, there is one other factor to keep in mind: How many FREE enrollments do you get. What do I mean by FREE? How many referrals do you get? How many walk-ins? How many family add-ons? How many from demos? How many from birthday parties? How many from other labor intensive, but non-advertising sources? If you get some of your enrollments from sources like these, then you could double the amounts that I discussed above and still remain within about 10% of your total gross going for advertising.

Example from number 2: If that school has an average lifetime student value of $4,000-plus, and they spent $800 for an enrollment from paid advertising sources — assuming that some of their enrollments were from free sources, then they would still average 10%, or $400 per enrollment, even if their student acquisition cost were $800 for paid advertising generated traffic.

Second, costs "at the margin," versus "the average." There is an interesting concept from economics that applies here. First, understand what we mean by "at the margin." If you spent $5,000 for the month on advertising, the next marginal expenditure is dollar-$5,001. Often times in marketing efforts, you may encounter "declining marginal return," In other words, for each additional dollar you spend, you get less and less return per dollar.

In a sense, this is what happens in every school starting with the first dollar spent.

Example: A school spends $0 on marketing and advertising in any given month. For that month they get give new students as referrals and two as walk-ins. They have eight new students at $0 direct costs. If they then spend $1,000 in advertising and get two additional students, they now have two more students at a marginal cost of $500 each. Their marginal cost per new student acquisition jumped from $0 to $500 immediately. Their average cost jumped from $0 to $200 per enrollment.

How much are you willing to pay at the margin?

Ultimately, look at that question like this one:

What is the most you would be willing to pay today in order to receive $4,000 over the next 33 months? Ultimately, at the margin, you should be willing to pay a relatively HUGE amount of money for one additional student.

Before we go any further, remember all of the above discussion depends upon the lifetime value of your student. This number includes all monies that that student will pay into your school, including down payments, exam fees, gross profit on retail items, monthly tuition payments and pre-paid tuition payments.

To get an easy approximation of this number for your school, take your year's gross and divide by the number of enrollments. That is: $500,000 gross divided by 250 enrollments equals $2,000 average value per student. If your numbers have been changing rapidly (especially if that means you are growing rapidly) take the last three years numbers and look at the sum from that longer-term perspective.

How do you get your lifetime value of a student up?

1. Greater RETENTION (more longevity within your students);
2. Higher tuition rate;
3. Lower family discounts for second, third and fourth family members;
4. More retail sales;
5. Find more things to sell your students (supplements, clothing, etc.).

Chapter 36

*Stepping Over Dollars to
Pick Up Pennies*

Chapter 36

Stepping Over Dollars to Pick-up Pennies

It's amazing to me sometimes what concerns school owners of small and barely profitable schools.

You see, there's a big difference between the way that successful school owners think about issues, big and small, versus how failures think about the issues in their business.

Recently, when speaking at the NAPMA Extreme Success Academy event, I was inundated with comments and questions from small school owners that belied two common problems:

1. A lack of an abundance mentality;
2. A focus on saving pennies rather than earning dollars.

First, most school owners have expectations that are way too low for their business, and lack faith in their own capabilities to achieve a high level.

They ask how to run their school more effectively, while holding a fulltime job in some other career. Rather than looking at the real potential of their business, they try to coordinate their day job to support their life-style needs, while also working at the school 40 hours a week.

While they are struggling along with their two jobs, other schools are thriving.

Just this month, three of my close friends had schools gross over $100,000 in a single month. They are spread out across the country, have different programs, different curriculum, different strategies for attracting new students and much different personalities. However, each of these school owners are not just surviving, they are thriving.

It is important for the school owners to make a decision that they are going to not just survive but, thrive in their school. School owners who are running their school on a part-time basis must decide to thrive, then "jump off the cliff" and run their school and a professional, full-time basis.

Second, saving pennies rather than earning dollars works in two specific ways.

First, doing everything themselves rather than farming out critical support items, school owners go through their daily routine looking a small incremental gains in their business, hoping to save a few dollars here and there.

School owners who are grossing $5,000, $7,500, $11,000 or $13,000 patiently explain how they are saving $1 or $2 per payment by doing their billing in-house, rather than farming it out to a service provider, or explain that they do all of their payroll and bookkeeping on their own, rather than pay the $60 or $70 per month that a service firm like Paychex or ADP would charge.

Focusing on items like billing, payroll, accounting and taxes takes up valuable time that could better be spent on the important elements of growing a school.

Every school owner must master three key elements for their school:

1. Marketing to generate new students
2. Sales, enrollment processes and renewal or upgrade processes
3. Motivational teaching

These three elements must be attended to effectively every day.

Really the owner's main role is in marketing his school and then monitoring for quality student service. Everything else is secondary.

Second, failing to invest in crucial points for growth. Every school owner must spare no expense on two items:

1. His or her own education as a martial arts business person.
2. Marketing and advertising their school.

When speaking with owners of small schools, they often explain to me how attending a worthwhile seminar is just not in their budget. They just are not willing to spend $1,500 to $5,000 on their own education, even if they might learn enough to make 10 or 20 times the investment. Often, I see even a more perverse spin on this, where martial artists will spend huge amounts of money on curriculum-oriented training developing their own athletic talents, but those same individuals fail to see the value of business education to support their school's growth.

Next, the most frustrating aspect of attempting to teach school owners about marketing is their lack of willingness to invest effectively in the growth of their own school. Proven concepts with a 3 to 1, 5 to 1or even 10 to 1 return on investment are ignored or derided as too expensive or too ineffective. Smaller school owners often combine unrealistic expectations with a lack of willingness to invest effectively.

In conclusion, we are in a wonderful business. The more students we have and the more effectively we develop our students, then the more income we will earn. Financially successful school owners are impacting high numbers of students in a very positive way.

In order to grow your school you must have a belief in the opportunity provided by your school and be willing to invest in both your own education as well as in marketing your school.

Chapter 37

"The Pulse of a School"

Chapter 37

"The Pulse of a School"

In recent columns I have referred to the "success formula below. In this column I want to address the "pulse" of a school. How does this apply? Well, it certainly affects retention rates and renewal rates, and should affect referrals (i.e., enrollments) as well.

New Enrollments X Tuition Rate X Retention Rates X Renewal Up-sells X Cash Ratio

What do I mean by the "pulse" of a school?

Well, over the years I have figured out that I can pretty much judge the success level of a school within about five minutes during "prime-time." How and what do I mean?

Well, let me share a story to illustrate.

Many years ago, possibly 1985 or 1986, I traveled to Syracuse, NY, to visit a school run by a good friend by the name of Steve LaVallee. Why did I travel from beautiful Denver, Colorado to dreary Syracuse just to visit a martial arts school?

Well, Steve had a school in Liverpool (suburb of Syracuse) that was 1,800-square-feet on the second floor, with about $600 per month in rent, that was running 500 or more active students and spinning off literal wheelbarrels full of money. It was possibly the school with the lowest overhead and highest %age — and, maybe even total — net profit that I had seen before or since.

During the trip with a couple of my key staff members, we drove up to the school, which was in a really dingy area with no convenient place to part, and had to search a little to find the school. We walked up to the school, and there was a really strange heavy steel door with an embossed dragon and some other strange design (Steve loved that door!).

We opened the door at about 5 p.m. There was a narrow staircase up to the second floor.

I turned to one of my staff members and said something to the effect of, "I really don't need to see anything else. I already know why this school is so successful."

What was the secret? Well let me describe the scene.

All of the windows were fogged up. The noise level was deafening. Parents were sandwiched between students stretching out in preparation for the upcoming class. The class was divided into four pods. One fourth of the class at any time was working on a section of a Kenpo form, while three fourths of the class was standing in a horse stance around the perimeter counting and doing a blocking drill (with very little room for their minimal movement).

During our evening at the school, his program director left the office only to find the next parent and student to enroll or renew, and literally was in enrollment or renewal conferences for four hours straight with no let-up. Their rather cute receptionist had one finger in her ear, and the other on the volume enhanced headset, confirming intro appointments, renewal appointments and following up on anyone who had missed a class or a week of classes.

The personality of the school and the energy in the environment was unmistakable. The positive outlook, positive messages shared by the instructors, and the perpetual movement was incredible. There was as Tom Peters would say, an incredible "WOW" factor.

All night parents brought their friends, and students brought their associates, to witness the incredible energy and excitement of the school.

To top it off, when we rented a car, stopped for lunch, or went out for dinner, EVERYONE knew of LaVallee and his incredible school.

Everyone we talked to had a friend or relative in the school, or had trained there, or intended to train there soon.

At the end of the day, I decided to tease Steve a little — after all, I was also having pretty good success in Denver. I teasingly said, "Gee, Steve, with the barrels of money you are hauling out of this school, it seems like you could afford real mirrors." Well, see, he had the only wall that didn't house spectators covered with one-foot by one-foot mirror tiles, not plate-glass mirrors. You couldn't possibly watch yourself do anything in the mirrors because of all the wacky angles.

He smirked and said, "No, no, you don't understand," and led me to a closet what was filled with several boxes of the mirror tiles. I said, "Okay, fine you bought too many. What's the big deal?" "No, No," he said, "Watch the guys cleaning up now after class."

Well, I turned, and in amazement watched his instructor scrape three broken tiles off the wall and replace them with new ones from the closet.

He said, "See, we have so many people crammed in here, we break several every night. These are much easier to replace than a 6-foot plate glass." He then piled several thousand dollars into a gym bag with his 357 magnum, and tossed it lovingly under the hood of his convertible 911 before attempting to set a new land speed record on the way home.

Chapter 38

Are You a Professional?

Chapter 38

Are You a Professional?

I feel that unfortunately, very few of the many thousands of martial artists who read this really think of themselves as professionals, even those who do, rarely behave that way on a consistent basis.

Although there are a few "professional athletes" in our industry, they are few and far between. Maybe some of the current fighters are able to make an adequate living using strictly their fighting skills. Things really haven't changed much since 1980, when I changed my personal view of what the word "professional" would mean to me in Martial Arts.

A short story: In 1980 and 1981, I was attending Georgetown University, and working with Charlie Lee, John Chung and a big stable of "professional" fighters. That stable was part of the Jhoon Rhee Institute, and included my teacher, friend and mentor Jeff Smith, who was the World Champion, as well as Rodney Batiste (U.S. Champion), Mike Coles (U.S. Champion), and a bunch of up-and-comers — and, a few wannabe's.

We were in the unique situation of hosting ESPN-televised fights about every other month, sanctioned by Joe Corley's PKA, and of having a student base of a couple of thousand eager students buying tickets to the fights held in one of Jhoon Rhee's schools (a monstrous 13,000-square-foot school, boxing gym, kickboxing training center and events center wrapped into one).

I ended up in Washington, D.C. (actually I was living in Jeff Smith's condo across the street from the Pentagon in Crystal City, VA), to train to be a professional fighter, and to get a degree in Economics on the way to an MBA. During my time in Washington, I learned some interesting, and at the time, disappointing lessons.

The first lesson that I learned was the meaning of "professional" as it applied to athletics. The training regime that was required of Jeff Smith and the other fighters in our stable was truly incredible compared to martial artists that were not professionals. Each of our world-class fighters had a huge regiment of roadwork, weight training, time in the boxing gym with trainer Jimmy Jones and time in the kickboxing gym working on jump rope, shadow sparring, medicine ball and bag work. This didn't include the many "rounds" of sparring that proceeded any significant fight. I was soon to discover that it was impossible for me to train as a "professional fighter" and be an

"A" student at a top-10 school like Georgetown, and to be a "professional martial arts teacher."

The next difficult lesson that I learned is that being a professional fighter is a difficult, dangerous, and unlikely career. At the time, Bill Wallace, Jeff Smith, Joe Lewis, Jean Yves-Theriault and Don Wilson were at the top of their games. I was soon to realize that most "professional" fighters were earning $100 to $200 per round, and even the World Champions were unable to make much of a living through fighting alone. Most supplemented their income, either through seminars, or by "professionally" running martial arts schools.

In watching and learning from Jeff Smith, I quickly figured out that he and Jhoon Rhee and Nick Cokinos were driving nice cars, living in beautiful homes, and generally enjoying an excellent lifestyle from running martial arts schools. Jeff was careful to keep his fighting from interfering with his real career of running profitable martial arts schools. I learned in 1980 that a career as a professional martial arts teacher was much more likely than a career as a professional fighter, and, frankly, much more lucrative.

Having learned that "professionalism" was in the preparation and training, not just in the execution, I quickly shifted attention and decided to be a professional in every way in my career from that day forward. I decided to move to Denver to open professional martial arts schools. I began training to be a professional school owner. That meant studying everything available about running a professional business and school. For two years I studied with Jeff Smith, Nick Cokinos, Jhoon Rhee, Ned Muffley and others about how to really run a profitable school.

Next, I "camped out" at the Library of Congress, and read everything I could get my hands on about advertising, direct marketing and sales, as well as general business operations. Then, I learned that the FTC was having hearings on health spas, so I spent several months going through the millions of pages of documents on file and read the sales manuals, sales manager's manuals and club operations manuals for every major health club in the country.

For good measure I took every class offered by the Small Business Administration and by SCORE on business operations. Finally, I spent nine months working with a start-up school to learn the ins and outs of how to start a new school effectively.

Finally, after all that, I put together a 200 page business plan, moved to Denver and opened five schools in 18 months with $10,000 in capital. In the past 20 years, I have earned a Master's in Business, read 20 to 30 books (sometimes more) on some aspect of running a professional school (i.e. education, sales, marketing, management, etc.) each year, often spend $50,000 or more a year training myself and my staff, and continue to study the best schools in the country and model similar businesses in other fields.

My question is this. Do YOU train yourself as a professional as a school operator? If not, why not?

Chapter 39

*How Does a Mile High Karate
School Generate Revenue?*

Chapter 39

How Does a Mile High Karate School Generate Revenue?

The total revenue of a Mile High Karate school will be affected by several factors. In simple terms, the revenue flow ends up being a function of:

New Enrollments X Tuition Rate X Retention Rates X Renewal Up-sells X Cash Ratio

To simplify this, picture the average path that a student may take through the business side of a Mile High Karate school.

First: The family is exposed to Mile High Karate in one of a variety of ways. They may first come in contact with us by responding to one of our regional ads in the *Rocky Mountain News* or *Denver Post*, from our infomercial, or they may be responding from a localized ad such as direct mail or Val-Pak. Often, they are either a participant in one of our many community outreach programs, or are referred by an existing student. Regardless of the source, they enter our introductory process, and hopefully, 35% to 65% of the time, end up enrolling in our "trial enrollment," which is for a year.

They either pay an average of $259 to enroll then and $159 per month (our schools currently range from $139 to $189 per month for this program), or they pay one payment averaging $1,700 (there are small family discounts for a second and third family member of 10 and 20%, respectively.)

Second: The student enters our White Belt class, where they train twice a week for eight to twelve weeks. During that time, they are being prepared for and evaluated for our Black Belt training. Prior to testing for Gold Belt (at the end of the eight to twelve weeks), they are evaluated for, and, if they qualify, offered the opportunity to join the Master Club (a higher level of training

that point, if they join Master Club — which 35 to 50 % should do at this point — they will either pay $500 down and have an approximately $100 increase in their monthly payment, or will pay one payment averaging $7,800, again with 10 tor 20% discounts for a second and third family member.

Third: The student enters our Beginner Class (Gold, Orange, Green and Purple Belts), and either trains as a new Master Club member (with additional class times and opportunities and teams they can participate in at that level) ,or as a Gold belt for two months, and continue to revisit the qualification process to Master Club. Most of those who have not yet joined Master Club will prior to the Orange Belt test, although some%age never will, and will continue on to the trial level.

Additionally, upon entering the beginner's class, each student will purchase a variety of equipment, including hand pads, foot pads, head gear, shin pads, rib guard and some of the basic weapons required by curriculum. In total, a student will purchase between $150 and $200 in equipment (our cost varies from 35% to 50% of the retail price of these sales).

Fourth: The students continue to train through Beginner, Intermediate and Advanced classes. During the process, there will be an inevitable%age of the students who will drop out without completing whichever program they have enrolled to complete.

Our schools have encountered a low of 2% monthly attrition to a high of 7%. Our target range is 3.5% or less per month. This varies monthly based upon a variety of factors, some seasonal, such as Christmas Season or Summer, and based upon instructional quality and parent-student rapport levels with the teachers and other staff.

In determining the monthly revenue stream of the school we categorize revenue streams as follows:

Tuition

Enrollment Down Payments
> $259 first student in family, $239 second member, $219 third member — average tuition.

Enrollment (1 year) Paid-In-Fulls
> $1,700 on average.

Renewal Down Payments
> ($500, 1st family member; 10 to 20% family discounts. This number varies.

Renewal Paid-In-Fulls
> $7,800 first person, 10 to 20% off additional family members.

Monthly Tuition Payments
> Billed through Mile High Events by ASF via EFT or Credit Card: $159, $139, $119 first, second, third family members; $100 more Master Club.

Retail Sales
Pads, Uniforms, Weapons, Books, etc.

Chapter 40

*How I Opened Five Schools
in 18 Months with $10,000
When I was 23*

Chapter 40

How I Opened Five Schools in 18 Months with $10,000 When I was 23

In a previous chapter, "Are you a Professional?," I discussed the extensive preparation that I went through prior to opening my schools 20 years ago. In this chapter I would like to give you an overview that you can use today of howI opened 5 schools in 18 months with only $10,000.

Prior to opening: Extensive training on business operations, extensive market research to locate a "good market," i.e., demographic research to target adequate income levels, population densities and proper age breakdowns and effective lease negotiations (I wanted build-out dollars and FREE rent early in the deal).

Then open the doors and do the following:

Step 1: All start-up capital into MARKETING.

Step 2: 100 enrollments in 6 weeks.

Step 3: Renew everyone on their second or third month.

Step 4: Get them to pay CASH.

Step 5: Use that cash for two things: Facility improvements and to open location number two.

Step 6: Continue to repeat this cycle.

Now, I know that I make this sound simple, and, really, it isn't. But, there are some key ingredients that I believe that most new schools miss.

First: Growing slowly as a start-up means either burning through lots of cas,h or without lots of cash to burn through, means going out of business. Or, often it means, in our industry, support your hobby (i.e., running a school) with your career (i.e., your day job).

I had very little money and no other source of income for myself, my wife and my full-time instructor. This thing had to create cash, in a hurry, or disaster would strike.

Second: "If you build it, they will come," may work in Kevin Costner movies, but nowhere else.

It's more like, *if* you build it, advertise, promote, beat the bushes, knock on doors, hone your sales skills, close everyone who comes within three feet of you, and, hustle…hustle…hustle, they will come. Facilities are important to properly support a large student body, and almost irrelevant to growing one to begin with. I've seen way too many schools rent a huge space, spend every last cent on mats, bags, mirrors, inventory and state-of-the-art training gear, then wait and hope for someone to come and train.

Third: Now, don't miss the message: To get enrollments, a good first impression is important. To create prospects, good demographics are essential, and a highly-trafficked center or high-visibility certainly doesn't hurt. However, you grow your school by generating prospects, having strong closing ratio to enrollments and good student retention. These are affected by marketing, sales and teaching skills — nothing else matters much.

Fourth: Create CASH FLOW in a hurry. The model of a low down payment, long monthly payments and no cash enrollments or renewals means you are going to either BURN THROUGH LOTS OF CASH, or GO OUT OF BUSINESS. Every school I opened had POSITIVE CASH-FLOW in month one. How do you create positive cash flow? Big down payments, cash enrollments and cash renewals. Nothing else.

Fifth: Be good at what you do before opening the doors. You've got to know how to market your school, how to handle the intros and the enrollment process, and how to flip them quickly to renewals. On-the-job-training means you are going to either BURN THROUGH LOTS OF CASH or GO OUT OF BUSINESS.

Sixth: "Bootstrap." I projected prior to opening that I needed $50,000 to open a new school properly. I had a partner lined up. I had the research, knowledge and skills. He had the money. Well, after I put together the business plan, moved to Denver, and located the first location, he backed out. Now I had the knowledge, but no money. After being turned down by every bank I approached, my parents invested $10,000, and I opened with one-fifth the amount of money my well-thought out business plan projected that I needed. I plunged ahead, essentially "burning the boats" behind me, and had no choice but to make it work.

Seventh: "Lean and Mean." Control your expenses. Many start-up schools (and more established schools) ramp their expenses up way beyond what is reasonable for their revenue and their active student count. Someone needs to do the selling, and someone needs to teach the classes. It is very difficult for that to be one person. Beyond that, you don't need much staff early on, and when you add staff, they are inexpensive (i.e., someone to answer the phones or clean the bathrooms).

Eighth: Reach out to your community. There is an excellent trend in our industry towards growth through referrals alone. Now, that's great if you have 300 active, but what if you have 0, 25 or 50? That's not going to get you to 100 in six weeks, or 300 in five or six months.

Finally: "Plunge ahead Boldly." Tentative efforts lead to tentative results. Make a decision to be committed to success, then apply 100% of your energies towards accomplishing that goal.

Oh, by the way. Do I recommend you do five schools in 18 months as I did? NO WAY! However, these lessons work for opening one school, or dramatically growing your existing school.

Chapter 41

The Formula for Financial Success

Chapter 41

The Formula for Financial Success

This is a powerful formula that I have shared with you already while discussing how a Mile High Karate school generates revenue. Here I will expand upon that formula. The formula again is as follows:

New Enrollments X Tuition Rate X Retention Rates X Renewal Up-sells X Cash Ratio

I believe, that properly applied, this formula encompasses just about every important factor in improving the financial results of your school. An improvement in any piece of this formula can have a dramatic impact on your "bottom line net profit," and on your "top-line revenue."

Let's take a quick look at three of these factors: **Retention Rates**, **Renewal Up-sells** and **Cash Ratio.**

There has been a creeping mythology by some of the billing companies that accepting cash up front, as opposed to a monthly payment, is a bad, or even illegal, activity. This goes right along with the myth that students should enroll at a given price per lesson or month, and just go right along paying that rate forever (which, of course, means until they dropout).

There is a huge problem with the philosophy of never accepting cash: Students drop out.

Certainly one factor — but, only one — in the long-term financial health of a school, is minimizing student attrition (drop-outs). The industry average for dropout rates probably ranges from 7 to 10% per month. Now, to give you a comparison, I did a little research, and found that Harvard University (not known for it's easy curriculum) has a graduation rate of 93%. Put differently, Harvard has seven% of incoming freshmen will drop out sometime in the four- or five-year process of getting their degree. 93% of those

incoming freshmen will hang in there all the way to get their degree.

What would happen if you could get your school to a 93% graduation rate to Black Belt? If you enrolled 250 new students this year, you would graduate over 225 Black Belts in four years.

The absolute BEST dropout rate I've been able to find in our industry is around two% per month, or approximately 100% by the end of four years. Compare this to Harvard's seven% by the end of four years. Again, I believe that our industry average ranges from 7% to 10% PER MONTH dropping out.

If the numbers I've just quoted are anywhere near accurate, this leads us to two conclusions:

First: If someone pays you upfront for three or four years ahead, then there will be a bump in revenue as opposed to them paying monthly over that same period of time.

Second: A huge opportunity for improvement in all martial arts schools is figuring out how to extend the average length of time that a student continues to train in your school. Dropping the attrition rate monthly from 7% to 3.5% per month will DOUBLE your active count, and boost your revenue per student dramatically.

Next: The Renewal Up-sell

If you are a good martial arts instructor, do you think that it is possible to build a perception of value over a couple of months that exceeds their perception after one or two introductory lessons? It seems obvious to me that if your program is high quality, and if your instructors are good, then a student, after a couple of weeks or a couple of months, should be more tuned into the value of instruction, then on their initial couple of visits.

Also, in the long-term of your program, is the value of a white belt lesson comparable to the lesson a Black Belt would receive?

Maybe going back to my example from academics: Is tuition for a quality private high school, BA level college classes, Master's level college classes, and a Ph.D. program, of comparable value? Do they price them the same? If you don't know, the price per class hour typically escalates significantly at each step up, and at the same time, the number of students at each level typically declines significantly. When I completed my MBA, it was an executive program, only accepting individuals with a minimum of 10 years in management experience. The director of the program gleefully explained that we were in the highest profit per student program at the university.

A very successful school operator that I knows works it out like this: Basic course (new enrollment) $120 per month; Black Belt Course: $150 per month; Master Club: $175 per month; and Leadership program: $200 per month.

At Mile High Karate, we do it this way: New enrollment: $159 per month; Master Club: $250 per month.

To sum up this initial overview:

First: Go to work on your student retention rates. Make every effort to extend the average training time of each student.

Second: Have a renewal up-sell that you implement quickly into their enrollment — 2–4 months. That renewal program should bump up their tuition. Give them a cash option with some incentives to pre-pay the tuition.

Third: Target a fairly high%age of cash programs at the renewal. We target 35% or more cash at Master Club. It boosts our average revenue per student, and gives those students more incentive to continue training to the completion of their Black Belt.

Chapter 42

A $1,000,000.00 Watch and Other Tales of Entrepreneurship

Chapter 42

A $1,000,000.00 Watch and Other Tales of Entrepreneurship

Many years ago, I had the worst year of my business career.

The Denver economy collapsed, my marriage disintegrated, most of my staff quit in mass, I ended up broke and over $250,000.00 in debt, and generally at wit's-end.

This followed international recognition for being the fastest growing school chain ever and I was in demand internationally for my sage advice — yet in the meantime my business, and my life conspired to implode all at once.

Following a year like that, it is typical that your self-esteem and confidence may be shattered. All of the beliefs that you held regarding your own competence disappear, and in their place is a kind of shell-shocked groping for mediocrity. Following a proper mourning period, I decided that my reaction would not be as I described, but that I would come back bigger and better than ever.

That's when I started to search for some personal reward or goal that I could reward myself with upon success — something that would signify my return to the level of success that I had previously experienced and expected. Now, don't let me fool you. When you are broke and in debt to the tune of $250,000, financial survival might be a huge goal. But, that was not what I was after. I was after a huge return.

So I started looking for something, and after thinking about houses and cars, decided upon a relatively cheap, but outrageously decadent, incentive of a solid 18-carat gold Rolex Presidential Day-Date. Now, in the scheme of things, a watch isn't that big of deal, but $10,000-plus for a gold watch when you're broke seems like shooting for the moon.

I went to the jewelry store and gave them $500 (that I didn't really have to spare) to put the most expensive watch in the store on layaway. At the same, time I made a deal with myself that I could only have it if Mile High Karate did $1,000,000 or more that year. To call $1,000,000 a stretch goal is understating the situation, but that was what I determined to achieve. Now that I had the target ($1,000,000) and the deadline (by the end of that year), I had to get busy and figure out how to get there.

I spent several weeks putting together the "action plan." I reviewed our "stats" for the previous year in detail, and, boy, was that depressing. I looked for strengths, problems, opportunities and areas that needed minor tuning.

Then I figured out on a month-to-month basis what we needed to do in enrollments, new monthly payments, renewals and cash to hit my objective by the end of the year.

My next step was to review the staff that I had in place spread out among six locations, and size up their strengths and weaknesses, then to design a training and motivation plan to create my target performance among those people.

The first step was to break the $1,000,000 down into bite-size chunks for each school ,and to set monthly and quarterly targets through consultation with each school manager that they could really believe in. Next, I reviewed incentive and bonus plans, to give adequate incentive to each of my managers for their own performance.

Then, it came time to do two things:

First: Train, Train, Train. I focused on dramatic improvements in the competencies of each of my staff members. We drilled and role-played endlessly on info calls, introductory classes, enrollment conferences, and renewal conferences. I instituted new Black Belt and Teacher classes, and pulled each staff member up to a new, higher level of competency.

Second: I created graphs and charts and tracked our targets and actual results every Monday with a clear focus on enrollments, renewals, retention- and cash growth. What came next is aggressive, brutal, unflinching implementation. "Balls-to-the-wall" focused, making it happen, unabashed chaos of activity.

Did everything go smoothly and as planned?

Of course, not. I focused on a "whatever it takes" mentality, and actually had several staff members quit because they "didn't want to have to do whatever it takes," The "9–5" mentality strikes again. There were ups and downs, and frankly, we missed our target for three of the first four months of this "whatever it takes" plan. However, by keeping the goal in mind, ignoring the obstacles, and with bulldog-like tenacity, we plowed through my $1,000,000 goal by November 12th, and I immediately went and picked up my $1,000,000 watch.

By the way, the next year we hit $1.3 million, and the next year $1.8 million, and we kept on rolling. I bought the house down the street from my beautiful mountain retreat sold in the middle of divorce and crisis. I really was back!

Chapter 43

The Final Word...for Now

Chapter 43

The Final Word...for Now

A Journey Through a Martial Arts Business. When I started in martial arts over 32 years ago, or even as I worked my way through Georgetown University, I never would have imagined that martial arts instruction would become my profession, rather than just my passionate hobby.

When I founded Mile High Karate in 1983, it was an alternative to using my degree in International Economics to land in Banking, or to working for a corporate giant, such as Procter and Gamble or IBM. Instead, I moved from Washington, D.C. to Denver to open commercial martial arts schools.

My instructors and friends all thought I was crazy.

My key martial arts instructor gave me encouraging words that went something like this, "Well, you can play karate for a few years, then get a real job!" I'm sure you can imagine how satisfying it was to make them all "eat crow."

In the years since it's founding, Mile High Karate has achieved a truly international reputation for combining student quality with financial success. We've been the leading martial arts instruction organization in this region since inception.

At one time or another, I've been featured in all of the industry's trade publications, and have been a sought-after speaker and consultant throughout North America and the world. More recently, I've written several well-received books on martial arts school operations and teaching that have been well received throughout the United States and Canada, and as far away as New Zealand, Australia, Tokyo, UK, Germany and even, South Africa.

In Denver, Mile High Karate has taught over 25,000 students directly in our commercial facilities, and has introduced our program to kids in all of the major public and private schools, impacting well over 200,000 kids and their families in some small way. We've been featured on all of the major TV news programs and, in the local newspapers. We've even hosted Chuck Norris and other celebrities in the industry.

Honestly, when I pursued martial arts to a high level, it was as an athlete with intentions to follow in the path of my mentors, Jeff Smith, Pat Worley and others, to become a professional fighter and competitor. I was soon to grow out of that rather narcissistic focus and realize the potential for true significance through teaching. I'm certain that I'll never win another championship trophy in tournament competition, and many of my friends would humiliate me in seconds in a grappling match. However, that's not what I do as a career, or frankly, even as a hobby anymore.

My focus for Mile High Karate since the early 1980's has been elementary-age children, and their families. Teaching character, values, self-esteem, focus and goal-setting skills. We've developed a program that greatly enhances a child's achievement in school, and contributions at home and in their community. To further enhance that mission, Mile High Karate students have contributed to Children's Hospital, local public and private schools, and Chuck Norris' Kick Drugs Out of America organization.

Honestly, I can think of no other way to combine financial growth and security with true significant contributions to individuals, their families and the local community. Our direct impact on our students is huge, the ripple effect throughout our communities is immeasurable.

Many times in the past 20 years, I have been criticized for being "too commercial," "for being in martial arts 'only for the money.'" Or, for running "a Belt Factory," or, the "McDonald's of martial arts." To those critics I answer: I am in business to make money. I am in the Martial Arts Business because it combines the ability for me to make a satisfactory income with the ability to impact a huge portion of my community in a positive way. Honestly, I have the capability to make more money in some other industries, but not enough to encourage me to turn my back on what I love.

Why would I want to work in a career that I was less passionate about in order to support my martial arts school as a hobby? Alternatively, my

wealth from martial arts is only in proportion to the number of students I serve, and the depth of their enthusiasm for my service. Or, as Zig Ziglar is fond of saying, "You can get everything that you want in life, if you help enough other people get what they want."

Personally, I believe that the broader significance of a career as an educator far outweighs my own youthful enthusiasms for becoming a better fighter and high-end athlete. The personal satisfaction that grows from watching a beginner grow into a Black Belt and a shy and withdrawn child grow into a community leader makes all the difference in the world. I cannot imagine having spent the last 20 years selling real estate, marketing fast food or working in a corporate bureaucracy. I hope all martial artists will transition into this perspective. I hope many instructors will join my mission to expand our influence and develop a career that combines financial rewards, teamwork, family and contribution.

Stephen Oliver
Littleton, Colorato
2008

Made in the USA
San Bernardino, CA
27 July 2020